directory of PUBLISHING IN SCOTLAND 2007

directory of **PUBLISHING IN SCOTLAND** 2007

SCOTTISH **PUBLISHERS** ASSOCIATION

Directory of **Publishing in Scotland** 2007
First published in 1988

Fourteenth edition published in 2006 by:
Scottish Publishers Association
Scottish Book Centre
137 Dundee Street
Edinburgh
EH11 1BG

British Library Cataloguing in Publication Data
A record for this book is available from the British
Library

ISBN 10: 0 9548657 1 5
ISBN 13: 978 0 9548657 1 9

Cover design by Mark Blackadder
Text design by Mark Blackadder
Cover photograph by Graham Clark
Printed and bound in the UK by The Cromwell Press

Contents

Introduction

Lorraine Fannin, OBE

The Scottish Publishers Association (SPA) first produced a *Directory of Publishing in Scotland* in 1988 to answer the many daily queries received. Since that first edition, the *Directory* has changed from a simple booklet about the Scottish publishing industry, to a volume that includes helpful information about many aspects of the book business from a Scottish perspective. It also includes UK-wide information, where it is relevant and important. Now in its thirty-third year, we have again expanded the *Directory* to include a section on careers and a piece on the changing nature of the route to market for books.

We have also expanded the section on bibliographic data – giving timely and accurate information on new titles is key to achieving book sales. With the change to ISBN 13 on January 1st 2007, some notes on this are included.

The *Directory* offers information on: Scottish publishers and booksellers; literary prizes and awards; writers' groups; copyright and contracts; UK-wide training organisations and the Glasgow MLitt course; help on working as a freelancer; copy-editing and proofreading, and – for writers – how to prepare and submit typescripts, and an invaluable bibliography. You will also find information on individuals and companies who service the industry's needs, such as agents, designers, indexers, editors and printers.

We would like to extend our thanks to each individual, company and organisation listed for their support, and also to the readers and users who have contributed comments and suggestions for this edition. Liz Small edits the *Directory* and Katherine Naish and Ben Allan assisted this year.

Finally, and most importantly, we would like to thank John Turner and the Cromwell Press for their invaluable support of this publication.

Publishing in Scotland

Lorraine Fannin, Director, Scottish Publishers Association

The year ahead marks an interesting time for the Scottish publishing industry. Now in its thirty-third year, from a foundation of 12 publishers, to a current membership of c.70 companies, the Scottish Publishers Association is about to undergo a reorganisation in 2007 that will meet the needs of these challenging times.

With a transformation to a new kind of organisation and a much wider remit ahead of us, the changes are vital in this digital age where publishers can exploit all routes to market – be that via the Internet, DVD, games and/or books. With a new structure, the SPA – with a new name – will offer opportunities for organisations in the communications business, writers' groups and digital companies, to link to us, and join us... which means more networking, lobbying and more information resources for our current members, and our new members.

Despite many predicting the death of the book, UK book sales are strong. In 2005 the Scottish market was valued at an estimated £200 million (invoice value). And the Scottish book and journal publishing industry employs an estimated 1,250 people, with more freelance workers supplying services to the marketing, sales and distribution functions, as well as those working in editorial and production. Annually, we produce around 2000 new titles from Scotland, while in 2005 the overall UK book market produced 203,000 titles (more than the USA) and saw 11 new publishing companies start each week. In 2007 the world sees the ISBN go to 13 digits (from ten) because publishers' demand for ISBNs grows unabated, and the growth in downloadable academic chapters has meant ten digits are no longer enough.

The growth in the book sector is strong and, with *Richard and Judy*, readers' groups increasing in popularity, and stress laid on education, literacy, numeracy and lifelong learning, there is a strong national focus on reading. Nevertheless, in the UK a third of the population does not read at all, with one third buying only one or two titles a year (9.7 million books in 2005 were those authored by Dan Brown and J.K Rowling) and the remaining third classified as 'heavy book buyers'.

We live in the time of the Sony Reader, the iPod and downloadable content. Newspapers today can be downloaded in Warsaw or San Francisco with local adverts, and in June 2006 advertising spend on the Internet took over from newspaper advertising spend for the first time in the UK.

The SPA is changing to take on the challenges of publishers becoming 'content providers' and to ensure that creative talent throughout Scotland in the form of excellent photographers, illustrators, and a pool of committed freelance editors, designers and sales agents help the small publisher to compete commercially.

Bookselling is changing dramatically. Waterstone's and Ottakar's are now merging and those who buy our *Directory* year on year will notice that there is a much smaller independent book sector in Scotland. We greatly appreciate the support from our bookshops who have Scottish-interest sections, and most highlight the work of Scottish writers at regular intervals. We are pleased to be working so closely with the chains and independents in Scotland to create new opportunities for Scottish publishers, and very much value the relationship we have with Historic Scotland, VisitScotland and The National Trust for Scotland.

It is a sign of the times that in 2007 Tesco is on schedule to become the UK's third-biggest bookseller, and discounting and three-for-twos continue to be major themes in our lives. Other opportunities are presented by Google, who are digitising publishers' content for free in exchange for a deal of 20% of the content of their book, and by the technical wizardry which is developing both digital paper, fiction that is downloadable onto mobile phones, and in summer 2006 facilitated the launch of the Sony Reader. As ever there are many who prophesy the end of the book.

In December 2005 we celebrated the launch of the SPA e-commerce web site, after two years work, www.BooksfromScotland.com. This information-rich site now lists 13,000 Scottish-interest titles and gets 15,000 visits a month, with over a million hits to date. Growth of Internet use meant an explosion of interest for this useful and well-designed resource. BRAW, started up by Scottish Book Trust to promote Scottish children's writers and illustrators, (also) launched in 2005.

Changes in the publishing structure in this past year has seen Mainstream join the Random House Group, and Chambers the Hodder/Hachette group. There are many smaller companies too that have built up an impressive collection of work that reflects opportunities in the marketplace, and life in Scotland today.

The SPA's education group has focused on trying to find out gaps in the education market for extendable content from existing works from Scottish publishers, and has now conducted two questionnaires into the health of the Scottish education market for books.

In our work with Creative Industries, DCMS, our outreach work and networking links, we welcome the year ahead.

Scottish Publishers Association

Scottish Book Centre,
137 Dundee Street,
Edinburgh EH11 1BG
Tel: 0131 228 6866
Fax: 0131 228 3220
E-mail: firstname.lastname@
scottishbooks.org
Web site: www.scottishbooks.org
Date established: 1973

Contacts: Lorraine Fannin (Director);
Liz Small (Member Services and
Marketing Manager); Carol Lothian
(Finance and Administration);
Katherine Naish (Training and
Information Resources); Marion
Sinclair (Business Development),
Ben Allan (Personal and
Administrative Assistant)

Services offered: Information,
advice, consultancy, training, marketing, export and promotional services.
A description of the Association's
services to members is below.

Origins of the SPA

The Scottish Publishers Association
(SPA) was set up by a group of 12
publishers in 1973 as the Scottish
General Publishers Association, with
Robin Lorimer as the first chairman.
The Scottish Arts Council gave
financial support and the membership
grew. The membership at the time of
writing stands at 70 publishers and
the services offered are many and
varied. For most members, an
important element is the sharing of
advice and help, the recognition of a

common purpose at a time when the
whole industry faces change and
challenge, and an ability to combine
and pool resources to bring books
published in Scotland to the widest
possible market.

Who can become a member?

Full Membership of the SPA is open
to all companies and organisations in
Scotland that publish books for sale.
They should have published at least
two books by author(s) other than the
principals of the company; should be
offering the books for sale and should
be intending to develop a publishing
list. The publisher should be based in
Scotland. Companies who package
books normally join us as Full
members, and pay a subscription rate
based on their turnover, as do Full
members.

Associate Membership is open to
companies and organisations whose
aims are compatible with the SPA,
and who may be thought to derive
benefit from the Association, although
they may not have fulfilled the
membership criteria. Associate
members are not eligible for
nomination to the Council of the SPA.
The Council is elected annually by
and from the membership.

Library Membership is open to
libraries – public, academic and
specialist – which also publish
books or monographs. The link with
the publishing industry helps to bring
these organisations into contact
with designers, editors and a

marketing infrastructure.

Small Press Membership is a membership option for businesses or organisations starting up in publishing with an annual sales turnover below a commercial level and who wish to develop their expertise.

What are the aims of the SPA?

The Scottish Publishers Association aims to help publishers in Scotland to conduct their book-publishing business in a professional manner, to market their output to the widest possible readership within Scotland, the UK and overseas, and to encourage the development of a literary culture in Scotland.

What services does the SPA offer to members?

An annual programme of activities offers opportunities to all publishers, whatever their size, scope, speciality or geographical location. These activities are organised on a cooperative basis in order to save costs and administrative time. They include attendance at book fairs (home and abroad); marketing to bookshops, schools and libraries; publicity and advertising services; catalogue mailings and web site information; provision of professional training facilities in publishing skills; information resources and business advice. We also work on liaison with the UK bookchains.

In addition, the SPA implements research, develops projects and liaises with outside organisations which are considered to be of interest and benefit to the membership of the SPA, for example with The Publishing Training Centre, with universities, with the British Council, with the Scottish Executive and with Scottish Enterprise.

The following services are offered to all members of the SPA:

- Regular information bulletins about marketing opportunities, trade fairs, employment, manuscripts available, bookshops, overseas markets and general publishing news.
- Information and advice from the SPA's staff members and access to the SPA's library (see Bibliography pp.185-8).
- Access to services provided by export advisers, the Department of Trade and Industry, Scottish Trade International, and information on promotions, funding and advertising opportunities overseas.

Other services offered are charged at low rates. They include:

- Regular advance information and catalogue mailings to major bookshops, wholesalers, library suppliers and press contacts.
- New books information distributed to the UK book trade, media, libraries and individuals.
- Mailing labels from an extensive database.

- Representation at book fairs in the UK and abroad.

Members may display their books on the SPA stand even if they do not attend the fair personally.

Fairs have included:
Bologna Children's Book Fair
BookExpo America
Edinburgh International Book Festival
Frankfurt Book Fair
Gothenburg, Sweden
London Book Fair
Prague BookWorld
Scotland's International Trade Fair

- Promotional activities include joint advertising, press and media campaigns, book display facilities, new book catalogues, and web site events and book listings.
- Training courses and seminars on a wide range of publishing issues (also available to non-members).
- Export sales consortium to develop overseas sales.

Member publishers are also offered the services of BookSource, the distribution company, in which the SPA has a major interest.

How is the SPA financed?

Financial assistance comes from the Scottish Arts Council, subscriptions paid by members and charges made for services. These resources are constantly developed to bring improved benefit to the membership.

How is the SPA governed?

The SPA Council is the organisation's decision-making body, made up of representatives from twelve member publishers, elected by the membership at the AGM. Each Council member stands for an initial period of two years, after which they may offer themselves for re-election. Applications to join the SPA from publishers are reviewed by the SPA Council.

The following **Council members** were elected at the AGM on 15th September 2005:
Janis Adams (Chairman)
National Galleries of Scotland
Christian Maclean (Treasurer)
Floris Books
Neil Wilson (Vice-Chairman)
NWP Ltd

Council Members

Campbell Brown
Black & White Publishing
Fiona Brownlee
Mainstream Publishing
Kathleen Anderson
Canongate Books
Gavin MacDougall
Luath Press Ltd
Mike Miller
Geddes & Grosset Ltd
Lesley Taylor
NMS Enterprises Ltd – Publishing
Keith Whittles
Whittles Publishing

Scottish Publishers Association members

ACAIR LTD

7 James Street, Stornoway,
Isle of Lewis HS1 2QN
Tel: 01851 703020
Fax: 01851 703294
E-mail: info@acairbooks.com
Web site: www.acairbooks.com
ISBNs and imprints:
ISBN 10: 0 86152
ISBN 13: 978 0 86152
Company established: 1977
Titles in print: 400
Contacts: Norma Macleod
(Manager), Margaret Anne Macleod
(Design), Nina Moir (Administration)
Types of books published: All
categories of fiction and non-fiction
for children in the Gaelic language.
Adult books relating to the
Gaidhealtachd, history, music, poetry,
biography, environmental studies,
Gaelic language.
Distributor: BookSource,
50 Cambuslang Road
Cambuslang
Glasgow G32 8NB
Tel: 0845 370 0067
Fax: 0845 370 0068
Status of membership: Full

ASSOCIATION FOR SCOTTISH LITERARY STUDIES

Dept of Scottish Literature,
University of Glasgow,
7 University Gardens,
Glasgow G12 8QH
Tel/fax: 0141 330 5309
E-mail: office@asls.org.uk
Web site: www.asls.org.uk
ISBNs and imprints:
ISBN 10: 0 948877
ISBN 13: 978 0 948877
Company established: 1970
Titles in print: 40 plus journals
Contact: Duncan Jones
(General Manager)
Types of books published: Works
of Scottish literature which have been
neglected; anthologies of new
Scottish writing in English, Gaelic and
Scots; essays and monographs on
the literature and languages of
Scotland; comprehensive study
guides to major Scottish writers.

ASLS membership is open to all.
In 2006, a subscription of £38.00
(individuals) or £67.00 (corporate)
buys: one Annual Volume; New
Writing Scotland; Scottish Studies
Review (2 issues); ScotLit (2 issues);
Scottish Language (1 issue). Special
packages for schools and students
are also available.
Distributor: BookSource,
50 Cambuslang Road
Cambuslang
Glasgow G32 8NB
Tel: 0845 370 0067
Fax: 0845 370 0068
Status of membership: Full

ATELIER BOOKS

6 Dundas Street,
Edinburgh EH3 6HZ
Tel: 0131 557 4050
Fax: 0131 557 8382
E-mail: art@bournefineart.com
Web site: www.bournefineart.com
ISBNs and imprints:
ISBN 10: 0951; 1 873830
ISBN 13: 978 1 873830
Company established: 1987
Titles in print: 12
Contacts: Athina Athanasiadou
Types of books published: Books
on art and artists.
Distributor: BookSource,
50 Cambuslang Road
Cambuslang
Glasgow G32 8NB
Tel: 0845 370 0067
Fax: 0845 370 0068
Status of membership: Full

BARRINGTON STOKE LTD

18 Walker Street
Edinburgh EH3 7LP
Tel: 0131 225 4113
Fax: 0131 225 4140
E-mail: info@barringtonstoke.co.uk
Web site:
www.barringtonstoke.co.uk
ISBNs and imprints:
ISBN 10: 1 902260; 1 842990
ISBN 13: 978 1 903360;
978 1 842990
Titles in print: 270
Company established: 1997
Contacts: Sonia Raphael
(Managing Director)
Types of books published: Fiction
from award-winning authors for
children between the ages of 8 and
16 for dyslexic, struggling and
reluctant readers. Also FYI (fiction with
facts) and teacher, parent and
learning resources.
*We are unable to accept
unsolicited manuscripts*
Distributor: Macmillan Distribution
Ltd, Brunel Road, Houndmills,
Basingstoke, Hampshire RG21 6XS
Tel: 01256 329 242
Fax: 01256 812 521/558
E-mail: mdl@macmillan.co.uk
Status of membership: Full

BIRLINN LTD

(incorporating John Donald/Polygon)
West Newington House,
10 Newington Road,
Edinburgh EH9 1QS
Tel: 0131 668 4371
Fax: 0131 668 4466
E-mail: info@birlinn.co.uk
Web site: www.birlinn.co.uk
ISBNs and imprints:
ISBN 10: 1 874744 and 1 84158,
ISBN 13: 978 1 874744 *and*
978 1 84158 (Birlinn)
ISBN 10: 0 85976, 186232, 1898410
and 184017
ISBN 13: 978 085976, 978 1 86232,
978 1 898410 and 978 1 84017
(John Donald);
ISBN 10: 0 86241,
ISBN 13: 978 0 86241 (Canongate
A); *ISBN 10:* 07486, 1904598 and
09544,
ISBN 13: 978 0 7486, 978 1 904598
and 978 0 9544 (Polygon)
Company established: 1992
Titles in print: 750
Contacts: Hugh Andrew (Managing
Director), Andrew Simmons (Editorial),
Liz Short/Neville Moir (Production),
Helen Young (Sales), Jan Rutherford
(Publicity), Bob Smith (Key Accounts)
Types of books published: Scottish
classics and humour; local interest;
Gaelic; academic; Scottish history.
Includes John Donald and Polygon.

Distributor: BookSource,
50 Cambuslang Road
Cambuslang
Glasgow G32 8NB
Tel: 0845 370 0067
Fax: 0845 370 0068
Status of membership: Full

BLACK & WHITE PUBLISHING

99 Giles Street,
Leith,
Edinburgh EH6 6BZ
Tel: 0131 625 4500
Fax: 0131 625 4501
E-mail:
mail@blackandwhitepublishing.com
Web site:
www.blackandwhitepublishing.com
ISBNs and imprints:
ISBN 10: 1 873631; 1 84502,
0 9515151; 1 902927
ISBN 13: 978 1 873631;
978 1 84502; 978 1 902927;
978 0 9515151
B&W Publishing, CHROMA, Itchy Coo
Company established: 1990
Titles in print: 250
Contacts: Campbell Brown,
(Managing Director); Alison McBride
(Director); Gillian Mackay (Press
Officer); Janne Moller (Rights)
Types of books published: fiction;
true crime; sport; cookery; general
non-fiction; memoirs; Scottish
literature, history, biographies.
Distributor: BookSource,
50 Cambuslang Road
Cambuslang
Glasgow G32 8NB
Tel: 0845 370 0067
Fax: 0845 370 0068
Status of membership: Full

BROWN & WHITTAKER PUBLISHING

Tobermory,
Isle of Mull PA75 6PR
Tel: 01688 302381
Fax: 01688 302454
E-mail: OliveBrown@msn.com
Web site:
www.brown-whittaker.co.uk
ISBNs and imprints:
ISBN 10: 0 9528428; 0 9532775;
1 904353
ISBN 13: 978 0 9532775; 978 1
904353; 978 0 9528428
Company established: 1985
Titles in print: 18
Contacts: Olive Brown,
Jean Whittaker
Types of books published: Isle of
Mull, history, archaeology, wildlife,
genealogy, walking guides.
Distributor: Brown & Whittaker
Publishing
Status of membership: Full

CANONGATE

BROWN, SON & FERGUSON LTD
4–10 Darnley Street,
Glasgow G41 2SD
Tel: 0141 429 1234 (24 hrs)
Fax: 0141 420 1694
E-mail: info@skipper.co.uk
Web site: www.skipper.co.uk
ISBNs and imprints:
ISBN 10: 0 85174,
ISBN 13: 978 0 85174
Company established: c.1850
Titles in print: Over 500
Contacts: L Ingram-Brown (Joint
Managing Director), D H Provan
(Sales Manager)
Types of books published: Nautical
and yachting including Brown's
Nautical Almanac; the Nautical
Magazine; technical and non-technical
for sea literature; ship's stationery;
and model ship building; also one act
and full length plays; and Scout and
Guide publications.
Distributor: Brown, Son &
Ferguson, Ltd
Status of membership: Full

CANONGATE BOOKS
14 High Street,
Edinburgh EH1 1TE
Tel: 0131 557 5111
Fax: 0131 557 5211
E-mail: info@canongate.co.uk
Web site: www.canongate.net
ISBNs and imprints:
ISBN 10: 0 86241; 1 84195;
ISBN 13: 978 1 84195; 978 0 86241
Company established: 1994
(under present name)
Titles in print: 300
Contacts: Jamie Byng, Helen Bleck
(Managing Editor), Polly Collingridge
(Rights Director), Jessica Craig
(Associate Rights Director), Caroline
Gorham (Production Director), Jenny
Todd (Sales and Marketing Director),
Andy Miller (Editorial Director, Non-
Fiction), Anya Serota (Editorial
Director), Kathleen Anderson (Finance
Director)
Types of books published: Fiction;
biography; general non-fiction interest;
music, and Scottish interest.
We are unable to accept any
unsolicited manuscripts.
Distributor: Littlehampton Book
Services, Faraday Close, Durrington,
Worthing BN13 3RP
Tel: 01903 828510
Fax: 01903 828802
Status of membership: Full

Capercaillie Books

Chambers **HARRAP**

CAPERCAILLIE BOOKS LIMITED

1-3 Colme Street
Edinburgh
EH3 6AA
Tel: 0131 220 8310
Fax: 0131 220 8311
E-mail: info@capercailliebooks.co.uk
Web site:
www.capercailliebooks.co.uk
ISBNs and imprints: fairplay press
ISBN 10: 0 95429, 0 9545206,
0 9549625, 0 9551246
ISBN 13: 978 0 9551246
Contact: Kay Strang (Director)
Type of books published: Literary
criticism, contemporary Scottish
drama, Shakespeare, current affairs,
philosophy, culture.
Distributor: Gazelle,
White Cross Mills,
Hightown,
Lancaster LA1 4XS
Tel: 01524 68705
Fax: 01524 63232
Status of membership: Small Press

CHAMBERS HARRAP PUBLISHERS LTD

7 Hopetoun Crescent,
Edinburgh EH7 4AY
Tel: 0131 556 5929
Fax: 0131 556 5313
E-mail:
admin@chambersharrap.co.uk
Web site:
www.chambersharrap.co.uk
ISBN 10 and imprints:
0 550 Chambers; 0 245 Harrap
ISBN 13 and imprints: 978 0 550
Chambers, 978 0 245 Harrap
Company established:
Chambers 1832; Harrap 1901
Titles in print: 220
Contacts: Patrick White (Managing
Director and Publisher), Jane Camillin
(Sales & Marketing Manager), Ian
Scott (Production Manager), Clair
Simpson (Prepress Manager), Gerry
Breslin (Electronic Publishing
Manager), Mairead Hegarty (Key
Accounts Manager), Patrick Gaherty
(IT Manager), Elaine O'Donoghue
(Rights Manager)
Types of books published:
Publishers of the Chambers
Dictionary, Chambers offers a full
range of English dictionaries and
thesauruses; subject reference books;
language reference titles;
phrasebooks; crossword, puzzle and
Scrabble publications. Harrap –
French, Spanish, German, Italian and
Portuguese bilingual dictionaries and
study aids, plus a range of specialist
French and Spanish business
dictionaries.

Distributor: Macmillan Distribution Ltd, Brunel Road, Houndmills, Basingstoke, Hants RG21 6XS
Tel: 01256 302663
Fax: 01256 327961
E-mail: mdl@macmillan.co.uk
Status of membership: Full

CHAPMAN PUBLISHING LTD
4 Broughton Place,
Edinburgh EH1 3RX
Tel: 0131 557 2207
E-mail:
chapman-pub@blueyonder.co.uk
Web site: www.chapman-pub.co.uk
ISBNs and imprints:
ISBN 13: 978 0 906772;
978 1 903700
Company established: 1986
Titles in print: 30
Contacts: Joy Hendry (Editor);
Edmund O' Connor (Editorial Assistant)
Types of books published: Literary, arts and culture magazine; books – mainly poetry also fiction and drama. Submission instructions: Authors are usually drawn from those published in *Chapman* magazine. Send a letter detailing proposed publication, with an SAE for reply (or provide an e-mail address). Do not send unsolicited manuscripts.
Distributor: Chapman
Status of membership: Small Press

The Chartered Institute of
Bankers in Scotland

Chartered Institute of Library
and Information Professionals
in Scotland

CHARTERED INSTITUTE OF BANKERS IN SCOTLAND

Drumsheugh House,
38b Drumsheugh Gardens,
Edinburgh EH3 7SW
Tel: 0131 473 7777
Fax: 0131 473 7788
E-mail: info@ciobs.org.uk
Web site: www.ciobs.org.uk
Company established: 1875
Titles in print: 55
Contact: Giles Cuthbert
(Education Manager)
Type of books published: Banking
and business.
Distributor: Chartered Institute of
Bankers in Scotland
Status of membership: Full

CILIPS

(formerly Scottish Library Association)
Chartered Institute of Library and
Information Professionals in Scotland,
1st Floor Building C, Brandon Gate,
Leechlee Road, Hamilton ML3 6AU
Tel: 01698 458 888
Fax: 01698 283 170
E-mail: cilips@slainte.org.uk
Web site: www.slainte.org.uk
ISBNs and imprints:
ISBN 10: 0 900649
Company established: 2002
Contact: Elaine Fulton BA, MCLIP
(Director), Rhona Arthur (Assistant
Director), Alan Reid (Honorary
Publications Officer), c/o Midlothian
Libraries, Library HQ, 2 Clerk Street,
Loanhead, Midlothian EH20 9DR
Tel: 0131 271 3980
Fax: 0131 440 4635
Types of books published:
Librarianship, bibliographies, Scottish
interest, local and national history.
Distributor: BookSource
50 Cambuslang Road
Cambuslang
Glasgow G32 8NB
Tel: 0845 370 0067
Fax: 0845 370 0068
Status of Membership: Associate

COMHAIRLE NAN LEABHRAICHEAN/ THE GAELIC BOOKS COUNCIL

22 Mansfield Street,
Glasgow G11 5QP
Tel: 0141 337 6211
Fax: 0141 341 0515
E-mail: brath@gaelicbooks.net
Web site: www.gaelicbooks.net
and www.ur-sgeul.com
ISBNs and imprints:
ISBN 10: 0 951281
ISBN 13: 978 0 9512810
Company established: 1968
Titles in print: 7
Contact: Ian MacDonald (Director)
Types of books published:
Catalogues and book news
magazines; poetry posters.
Distributor: The Gaelic Books
Council
Status of membership: Associate

CONTINUING EDUCATION GATEWAY

199 Nithsdale Road,
Glasgow G41 5EX
Tel: 0141 422 1070
Fax: 0141 422 2919
E-mail: ceg@ceg.org.uk
Web site: www.ceg.org.uk
ISBNs and imprints:
ISBN 10: 1 902909
ISBN 13: 978 1 902909
Company established: 1989
Titles in print: 4
Contact: Linda Wilkie
Types of books published: Careers
and educational information books,
careers leaflets.
Distributor: Continuing Education
Gateway
Status of membership: Full

CUALANN PRESS

6 Corpach Drive,
Dunfermline,
Fife KY12 7XG
Tel/fax: 01383 733724
E-mail: info@cualann.com
Web site:
www.cualann.com
ISBNs and imprints:
ISBN 13: 978 0 9535036;
978 0 9544416
Company established: 1999
Titles in print: 18
Contact: Bríd Hetherington
Types of books published:
Scottish interest; history and
biography
Distributor: BookSource,
50 Cambuslang Road
Cambuslang
Glasgow G32 8NB
Tel: 0845 370 0067
Fax: 0845 370 0068
Status of membership: Small Press

DIONYSIA PRESS LTD

127 Milton Road West,
7 Duddingston House Courtyard,
Edinburgh EH15 1JG
ISBNs and imprints:
ISBN 10: 0 952234; 1 903171
ISSN: 0956 430
Company established: 1989
Titles in print: 44
Contact: Denise Smith (Director)
Types of books published: poetry
collections; translations; novels
Distributor: Dionysia Press
Status of membership: Small Press

DUDU NSOMBA PUBLICATIONS

5c Greystone Avenue, Rutherglen
Glasgow, G73 3SN
Tel: 0141 647 5195/ 07860629480
Fax: 0141 647 5195
E-mail: lwanda2000@yahoo.co.uk
Web site: www.pamtondo.com
ISBNs and imprints:
ISBN 10: 0 9532396; 0 9522233
Company established: 1993
Titles in print: 12
Contact: Dr John Lwanda
Types of books published: Literary;
historical; political; musical; general;
on Malawi or Africa
Distributor: Dudu Nsomba
Publications
Status of membership: Small Press

DUNDEE CITY COUNCIL

School Library Service
Central Library
The Wellgate
Dundee, DD1 1DB
Tel: 01382 431546
Web site:
www.dundeecity.gov.uk/library
Contacts: Stuart Syme,
Tel: 01382 431 546
E-mail:
stuart.syme@dundeecity.gov.uk
or Lynn Moy,
Tel: 01382 438 892
E-mail: lynn.moy@dundeecity.gov.uk
or Moira Foster
Tel: 01382 438 110
E-mail:
moira.foster@dundeecity.gov.uk
Types of books published: Dundee
City Council School Library Service
promote literacy and reading in
Dundee libraries and schools, and
initiated the Dundee City of Discovery
Picture Book Award in June 2006, and
published *Dundee Time Tram* about
the history of Dundee in August 2006,
for distribution to children in Dundee,
and trade sales.
Status of membership: Library

26

DUNEDIN ACADEMIC PRESS

Hudson House,
8 Albany Street,
Edinburgh EH1 3QB
Tel: 0131 473 2397
Fax: 01250 870920
E-mail:
mail@dunedinacademicpress.co.uk
Web site:
www.dunedinacademicpress.co.uk
ISBNs and imprints:
ISBN 10: 1 903765
ISBN 13: 978 1 903765
Company established: 2000
Titles in print: 30
Contacts: Anthony Kinahan
(Director), Norman Steven
(Finance Director)
Types of books published: Earth
sciences, ethnography and anthro-
pology, international affairs,
philosophy, education, health and
social care, history, religion and
religious affairs, singing and music.
We also distribute some titles
published by the Handsel Press.
Distributor: Turpin Distribution,
Pegasus Drive, Stratton Business
Park, Biggleswade, SG18 8TQ
Tel: 01767 604951
Fax: 01767 601640
Status of membership: Full

EDINBURGH CITY LIBRARIES/ DEPARTMENT OF CULTURE & LEISURE, CITY OF EDINBURGH COUNCIL

23-25 Waterloo Place,
Edinburgh EH1 3BH
Tel: 0131 529 7791
Fax: 0131 529 7846
E-mail:
head.of.libraries@edinburgh.gov.uk
Web site: www.edinburgh.gov.uk
ISBNs and imprints:
ISBN 10: 0 900353
Company established: 1890
Titles in print: 3
Contact: Bill Wallace
(Head of Libraries and Information
Services)
Types of books published: Books;
booklets; prints; greeting cards
Distributor: Edinburgh City Libraries
Status of membership: Library

EDINBURGH UNIVERSITY PRESS

22 George Square,
Edinburgh EH8 9LF
Tel: 0131 650 4218
Fax: 0131 662 0053
E-mail: editorial@eup.ed.ac.uk;
marketing@eup.ed.ac.uk
Web site: www.eup.ed.ac.uk
ISBNs and imprints:
ISBN 10: 0 7486; 0 85224
ISBN 13: 978 0 7486
Company established: 1948 EUP;
1992 EUP Ltd
Titles in print: 900 plus 25 journals
Contacts: Timothy Wright (Chief
Executive and Head of Journals),
Jackie Jones (Head of Book
Publishing), Ian Davidson (Head of
Production), Jan Thomson (Head of
Finance and Subscription Services),
Catriona Murray (Head of Sales and
Marketing), Stuart Midgley (Rights
Manager)
Types of books published:
Academic titles in social sciences and
humanities: Islamic studies; Classics
and ancient history; literature;
linguistics; philosophy; religious
studies; film and media studies;
American studies; politics; Scottish
history, politics and culture; gender
studies; history; sociology; African
studies.

Submission instructions:
submission of book proposals only;
send a maximum of two sample
chapters and a SAE.
Distributor: Marston Book Services
Ltd, PO Box 269, Abingdon,
Oxon OX14 4YN
Tel: 01235 465 500
Fax: 01235 465 556
Status of membership: Full

FLEDGLING PRESS LTD

7 Lennox Street (GF),
Edinburgh EH4 1QB
Tel/fax: 0131 332 6867
E-mail: zander@fledglingpress.co.uk
Web site: www.fledglingpress.co.uk
ISBNs and imprints:
ISBN 10: 0 9521579; 0 9544121
ISBN 13: 978 0 952179;
978 0 9544121;
New series: 978 1 905916 00 9 to
978 1 905916 99 3
Company established: 2000
Titles in print: 10
Contact: Zander Wedderburn
Types of books published: New
fiction; biography; specialist in web
publishing; e-books and short runs
Distributor:
Contact zander@fledglingpress.co.uk
Status of membership: Small Press

FLORIS BOOKS

15 Harrison Gardens,
Edinburgh EH11 1SH
Tel: 0131 337 2372
Fax: 0131 347 9919
E-mail: floris@florisbooks.co.uk
Web site: www.florisbooks.co.uk
ISBNs and imprints:
ISBN 10: 0 86315
ISBN 13: 978 086 315; 978 158 420
Company established: 1977
Titles in print: 370
Contacts: Christian Maclean
(Manager), Christopher Moore
(Commissioning Editor), Gale Winskill
(Children's Editor), Ulrike Fischer
(Production Editor), Angela Smith
(Publishing Assistant), Katy
Lockwood-Holmes (Sales and
Marketing Manager)
Types of books published: Celtic
studies; education; science; self-help;
mind, body and spirit; contemporary
children's; religion, craft and activity.
Submission instructions: Send a
synopsis only. We do not accept
children's picture book submissions.
Please see our web site for guidelines
on Kelpies submissions.
Distributor: BookSource,
50 Cambuslang Road
Cambuslang
Glasgow G32 8NB
Tel: 0845 370 0067
Fax: 0845 370 0068
Also distributor for Lindisfarne Press
Status of membership: Full

F O R T

**GEDDES &
GROSSET**   **WAVERLEY
BOOKS**

FORT PUBLISHING LTD

Old Belmont House
12 Robsland Avenue
Ayr KA7 2RW
Tel: 01292 880693
Fax: 01292 270134
E-mail: fortpublishing@aol.com
Web site: www.fortpublishing.co.uk
ISBNs:
ISBN 10: 0 9536576; 0 9544461;
0 9547431; 1 905769
ISBN 13: 978 0 9536576;
978 0 9544461; 978 0 9547431;
978 1 905769
Titles in print: 30
Company established: 1999
Contacts: James McCarroll
(Managing Director), Jane McCarroll
(Company Secretary)
Types of books published: History,
sport (especially football), crime,
photography, local interest, general
non-fiction
Distributor: Booksource Ltd,
50 Cambuslang Road
Cambuslang
Glasgow G32 8NB
Tel: 0845 370 0067
Fax: 0845 370 0068
Fax: 0141 557 0189
Status of membership: Full

GEDDES & GROSSET

David Dale House,
New Lanark,
Lanark ML11 9DJ
Tel: 01555 665000
Fax: 01555 665694
E-mail: info@gandg.sol.co.uk;
Web site:
www.geddesandgrosset.co.uk
ISBNs and imprints:
ISBN 10: 1 85534, 1 84205;
Geddes and Grosset;
1 902407, Waverley Books
ISBN 13: 978 1 84205, 978 1 85534
Geddes and Grosset;
978 1 902407 Waverley Books
Company established: 1987
Titles in print: Own imprint: 550
Contacts: Ron Grosset, Mike Miller
Types of books published:
Reference books; children's books;
regional interest books; calendars and
books as premiums.
Distributor: Geddes and Grosset –
Peter Haddock Ltd, Industrial Estate,
Pinfold Lane, Bridlington, Yorkshire
YO16 6BT
Tel: 01262 678121
Fax: 01262 400043
and Waverley Books – BookSource,
50 Cambuslang Road
Cambuslang
Glasgow G32 8NB
Tel: 0845 370 0067
Fax: 0845 370 0068
Status of membership: Full

Glasgow|museums

GLASGOW CITY LIBRARIES PUBLICATIONS

The Mitchell Library,
North Street,
Glasgow G3 7DN
Tel: 0141 287 2846
Fax: 0141 287 2815
E-mail:
maureen.wilbraham@cls.glasgow.gov.uk
Web site: www.glasgow.gov.uk
ISBNs and imprints:
ISBN 13: 978 0 906169
Company established: 1980
Titles in print: Over 30 with one as co-publisher and more than 20 library bibliographies.
Contacts: Maureen Wilbraham
Types of books published: Mainly Glasgow interest or related to material held in the Mitchell Library.
Distributor: The Mitchell Library
Status of membership: Library

GLASGOW MUSEUMS

Cultural and Leisure Services,
Glasgow City Council,
Martyrs' School,
Glasgow G4 OPX
Tel: 0141 271 8307
Fax: 0141 271 8354
E-mail:
susan.pacitti@cls.glasgow.gov.uk
Web site:
www.glasgowmuseums.com
ISBNs and imprints:
ISBN 10: 0 902752
ISBN 13: 978 0 902752
Company established: 1902
Titles in print: c.15
Contacts: Susan Pacitti
(Sales, Editorial, Publicity)
Types of books published: Art and guidebooks to collections, local history.
Distributor: Cultural and Leisure Services
Status of membership: Full

GOBLINSHEAD

GLENEIL PRESS, THE
& GLENEIL SPORTSMAN'S
PRESS, THE
Whittingehame,
Haddington,
East Lothian EH41 4QA
Tel/fax: 01620 860292
E-mail: gleneilpress@tiscali.co.uk
Web site: www.gleneil.com
ISBNs and imprints:
ISBN 10: 0 9525330
Company established: 1995
Titles in print: 9
Contact: Michael Brander (Editorial),
or at 01636 700585 Colin Harrison
(Sales)
Types of books published:
Scottish: historical; food; drink;
biography; humour; field sports.
Submission instructions:
Unsolicited manuscripts not returned
Distributor: BookSource,
50 Cambuslang Road
Cambuslang
Glasgow G32 8NB
Tel: 0845 370 0067
Fax: 0845 370 0068
Status of membership: Small Press

GOBLINSHEAD
130b Inveresk Road,
Musselburgh EH21 7AY
Tel: 0131 665 2894
Fax: 0131 653 6566
E-mail: goblinshead@sol.co.uk
ISBNs and imprints:
ISBN 10: 1 899874
ISBN 13: 978 1 899874
Company established: 1994
Titles in print: 33
Contact: Martin Coventry
Types of books published: Popular
and tourist books on Scottish history;
castles; biographies; architecture;
prehistory; Scottish fiction
Submission instructions: Scottish
interest, history, including fiction. No
submissions accepted until discussed
with staff. Please contact by e-mail
(goblinshead@sol.co.uk) or by phone.
Distributor: Goblinshead
Status of membership: Full

GW PUBLISHING

P O Box 6091,
Thatcham,
Berks RG19 8XZ
Tel: 01635 268080
Fax: 01635 269720
E-mail: graeme@gwpublishing.com
Web site: www.gwpublishing.com
ISBNs and imprints:
ISBN 10: 0 9535397; 0 9546701;
0 9551564
ISBN 13: 978 0 9535397;
978 0 9546701; 978 0 9551564
Company established: 1999
Titles in print: 15
Contact: Graeme Wallace
Types of books published: Popular
and tourist books on Scottish history,
pictorial guide books, calendars,
children's.
Submission instructions: by e-mail
to Graeme Wallace
Distributor: GW Publishing,
Bookspeed, Lomond Books and
Gardners Books
Status of membership: Full

HARPERCOLLINS PUBLISHERS

Westerhill Road, Bishopbriggs,
Glasgow G64 2QT
Tel: 0141 772 3200
Fax: 0141 306 3119
and 77–85 Fulham Palace Road,
London W6 8JB
Tel: 020 8741 7070
Fax: 020 8307 4440
E-mail: firstname.secondname@
harpercollins.co.uk
Web site: www.harpercollins.co.uk
Company established: 1819
Titles in print: c.10,000
Contacts: Victoria Barnsley (CEO
and Publisher), David Swartnick
(Group Sales and Marketing Director),
David Rye (Production Director)
Types of books published: Popular
and literary fiction; non-fiction;
biography; history; dictionaries and
reference; children's; bibles;
educational; sport; travel; home and
leisure; cartographic.
Distributor: HarperCollins Publishers
(Trade), Customer Services
Department, Campsie View,
Westerhill Road, Bishopbriggs,
Glasgow, G64 2QT
Tel: 0870 787 1722
Fax: 0870 787 993
Status of membership: Full

Hodder Gibson
Educational Publishers for Scotland

headline
publishing group

HODDER &
STOUGHTON

HODDER GIBSON

2a Christie Street,
Paisley PA1 1NB
Tel: 0141 848 1609
Fax: 0141 889 6315
E-mail: hoddergibson@hodder.co.uk
Web site:
www.hoddereducation.co.uk
ISBNs and imprints:
ISBN 10: 0 340; 0 7169
ISBN 13: 978 0 340; 978 0 7169
Company Established: 2002 (part
of Hodder Education), Hodder
Education established 1906, Robert
Gibson established 1874
Titles in print: Approx 270. 35 to be
published in 2006
Contacts: John Mitchell (Managing
Director), Katherine Bennett (Projects
Editor), Jim Donnelly (Scottish Sales
Manager), Elizabeth Hayes (Desk
Editor and Administration Executive)
Types of books published:
Educational textbooks and revision
guides for the Scottish curriculum.
Distributor: Bookpoint,
130 Milton Park,
Abingdon OX14 4SB
Tel: 01235 400 400
Status of membership: Full

HODDER HEADLINE SCOTLAND

2a Christie Street, Paisley, PA1 1NB
Tel: 0141 848 1609
Fax: 0141 889 6315
E-mail: bob.mcdevitt@hodder.co.uk
Web site:
www.madaboutbooks.co.uk and
www.hodderheadline.co.uk
ISBNs and imprints:
ISBN 10: 0 340,
ISBN 13: 978 0 340, 978 0 7472,
978 0 7553
Company Established: 2004
Contacts: Bob McDevitt (mobile
07876 508716)
Types of books published: General
(Fiction, crime, sport, biography,
history, TV tie-ins, science, business,
cookery) but not children's, religious
or educational titles.
Distributor: Bookpoint,
130 Milton Park,
Abingdon, OX14 4SB
Tel: 01235 400 400
Status of membership: Full

HOUSE OF LOCHAR

HOUSE OF LOCHAR
Isle of Colonsay, Argyll PA61 7YR
Tel/fax: 01951 200232
E-mail: lochar@colonsay.org.uk
Web site: www.houseoflochar.com
Titles in print: 55
Contacts: Kevin Byrne (Director),
Georgina Hobhouse (Editorial,
Sales)
Types of books published:
Scottish interest; history; art;
transport; topography, maritime and
fiction with a Scottish angle
Distributor: BookSource
Status of membership: Full

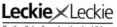

Leckie✕**Leckie**
Scotland's leading educational publishers

LECKIE & LECKIE PUBLISHERS
3rd Floor,
4 Queen Street,
Edinburgh EH2 1JE
Tel: 0131 220 6831
Fax: 0131 225 9987
E-mail:
enquiries@leckieandleckie.co.uk
Web site: www.leckieandleckie.co.uk
ISBNs and imprints:
ISBN 10: 1 84372; 1 898890;
0 9515718
ISBN 13: 978 1 84372;
978 1 898890
Company established: 1989
Titles in print: 150. Approx. 90 to
be published in 2007. (Digital
resources c.40)
Contact: Sarah Mitchell (Senior
Publisher), Alan Grierson (Publisher),
Richard Bass (Sales Manager), Rachel
Duncan (Marketing Executive)
Types of books published: Scottish
teaching, learning and revision.
Distributor: HarperCollins Publishers
(Trade), Customer Services
Department, Westerhill Road,
Bishopbriggs, Glasgow, G64 2QT
Tel: 0870 787 1722
Fax: 0870 787 1723
Status of membership: Full

LIPSTICK PUBLISHING
118 Dewar Street
Dunfermline
Fife
KY12 8AA
Tel: 01383 730 942
E-mail:
admin@lipstickpublishing.com
Web site:
www.lipstickpublishing.com
ISBNs and imprints:
ISBN 10: 1 904762
ISBN 13: 978 1 904762
Company Established: 2003
Contacts: Marie Lewis Stevenson
(Director)
Types of books published:
General.
Distributor: Booksource,
50 Cambuslang Road
Cambuslang
Glasgow G32 8NB
Tel: 0845 370 0067
Fax: 0845 370 0068
Status of membership: Full

LUATH PRESS LTD
543/2 Castlehill, The Royal Mile,
Edinburgh EH1 2ND
Tel: 0131 225 4326
Fax: 0131 225 4324
E-mail:
gavin.macdougall@luath.co.uk
Web site: www.luath.co.uk
ISBNs and imprints:
ISBN 10: 0 946487; 1 84282;
1 905222
ISBN 13: 978 0 946487:
978 1 842820; 978 1 905222
Company established: 1981
Titles in print: 150
Contact: Gavin MacDougall (Director)
Types of books published:
Committed to publishing well-written
books worth reading. Subjects
covered include: fiction; history;
guide-books; walking; skiing; poetry;
biography; natural history; current
issues and much more.
Submission instructions: Anything
from a tentative phone call to a
complete manuscript (including
introduction, author profile, synopsis
etc) welcome – we are delighted to
have the opportunity to discuss/
explore potential projects with any
individual or organisation, preferably
(but not exclusively) based in
Scotland.
Distributor: BookSource,
50 Cambuslang Road
Cambuslang
Glasgow G32 8NB
Tel: 0845 370 0067
Fax: 0845 370 0068
Status of membership: Full

MAINSTREAM PUBLISHING

MERCAT

MAINSTREAM PUBLISHING

7 Albany Street,
Edinburgh EH1 3UG
Tel: 0131 557 2959
Fax: 0131 556 8720
E-mail: gillian.bevan@
mainstreampublishing.com
Web site:
www.mainstreampublishing.com
ISBNs and imprints:
ISBN 13: 978 1 84596; 978 1 84018;
978 1 85158 and 978 0 906391
Company established: 1978
Titles in print: c.300
Contacts: Bill Campbell (Joint
Managing Director), Peter MacKenzie
(Joint Managing Director), Fiona
Brownlee (Marketing Director), Neil
Graham (Production Manager),
Sharon Campbell (Publicity Director),
Gillian Bevan (Sales Administration
Manager)
Types of books published: General
non-fiction; biography; autobiography;
art; photography; health; sport;
guidebooks; travel; true crime.
Submission instructions: Synopsis
and sample chapters in the first
instance. Supply a SAE or return
postage if manuscript is to be
returned.
Distributor: TBS, Frating Distribution
Centre, Colchester Road, Frating
Green, Colchester, Essex CO7 7DW
Tel: 01206 256000
Fax: 01206 255715
Status of membership: Full

MERCAT PRESS LTD

10 Coates Crescent,
Edinburgh EH3 7AL
Tel: 0131 225 5324/
Vikki Reilly 0131 225 9774
Fax: 0131 226 6632
E-mail: enquiries@mercatpress.com
Web site: www.mercatpress.com
ISBNs and imprints:
ISBN 10: 0 901824; 1 873644;
1 84183; 0 800 (ex-Aberdeen
University Press)
ISBN 13: 978 1 873644;
978 1 84183; Mercat Press, Crescent
Books (Fiction)
Company established: 1970
Titles in print: 300
Contacts: Tom Johnstone, Seán
Costello, Caroline Taylor (Editorial and
Marketing Assistant), Vikki Reilly
(Sales)
Types of books published: Books
of Scottish interest; biography; fiction;
history; outdoors & walking,
photography.
Distributor: BookSource,
50 Cambuslang Road
Cambuslang
Glasgow G32 8NB
Tel: 0845 370 0067
Fax: 0845 370 0068
Status of membership: Full

The NATIONAL
ARCHIVES
of SCOTLAND

NATIONAL
GALLERIES OF
SCOTLAND

NATIONAL ARCHIVES OF SCOTLAND (formerly SCOTTISH RECORD OFFICE)

HM General Register House,
2 Princes Street
Edinburgh EH1 3YY
Tel: 0131 535 1314
Fax: 0131 535 1360
E-mail: publications@nas.gov.uk
Web site: www.nas.gov.uk
ISBNs and imprints:
ISBN 10: 1 870874
ISBN 13: 978 1 870874
Company established: 1994
Titles in print: 40
Contact: Outreach Services
Types of books published:
General historical and educational publications designed to make the holdings of the National Archives of Scotland more accessible to amateur and professional researchers alike.
Submission instructions:
Unsolicited manuscripts are not accepted.
Distributor: Outreach Services Branch National Archives of Scotland
Status of membership: Full

NATIONAL GALLERIES OF SCOTLAND

The Dean Gallery,
Belford Road,
Edinburgh EH4 3DS
Tel: 0131 624 6257/6261
Fax: 0131 623 7135
E-mail: publications@ nationalgalleries.org
Web site: www.nationalgalleries.org
ISBNs and imprints:
ISBN 10: 0 903148; 0 903598;
1 903278
ISBN 13: 978 1 903278
Titles in print: 80
Contact: Janis Adams (Head of Publishing), Christine Thomson (Editorial, Sales), Ann Laidlaw (Administration), David Simpson (Editorial, Publicity)
Types of books published: Fine art and photography.
Distributor: Antique Collectors' Club
Status of membership: Full

National Library
of Scotland

NATIONAL LIBRARY OF SCOTLAND

George IV Bridge,
Edinburgh EH1 1EW
Tel: 0131 623 3700
Fax: 0131 623 3701
E-mail: enquiries@nls.uk
Web site: www.nls.uk
ISBNs and imprints:
ISBN 10: 0 90222, 1 872116
ISBN 13: 978 1 872116
Company established: 1925
Titles in print: 10
Contacts: Julian Stone (Marketing and Communications Officer)
Types of books published:
Bibliographies; facsimiles; catalogues; literary and historical books (usually in collaboration with other publishers).
Distributor: National Library of Scotland
Status of membership: Library

NEIL WILSON PUBLISHING LTD

Suite 303,
The Pentagon Centre,
36 Washington Street,
Glasgow G3 8AZ
Tel: NWP – 0141 221 1117
Fax: 0141 221 5363
E-mail: info@nwp.co.uk
Web site: www.nwp.co.uk
ISBNs and imprints:
ISBN 13: 978 1 897784;
978 1 903238; The In Pinn, Vital Spark, The Angels' Share, 11:9, NWP
Company established: 1992
Titles in print: 124
Contact: Neil Wilson (Publisher)
Types of books published: Whisky, food and drink, travel memoir, climbing and hillwalking, Scottish humour, biography, history, Irish interest and true crime.
Distributor: BookSource,
50 Cambuslang Road
Cambuslang
Glasgow G32 8NB
Tel: 0845 370 0067
Fax: 0845 370 0068
Status of membership: Full

NEW IONA PRESS, THE

Ardival Bungalow,
Strathpeffer, Ross-shire, IV14 9DS
Tel/fax: 01997 421 186
E-mail: mairimacarthur@yahoo.co.uk
ISBNs and imprints:
ISBN 10: 0 9516283; 0 9538938
ISBN 13: 978 0 9538938
Company Established: 1990
Titles in print: 6
Contact: Mairi MacArthur
Types of books published: Local
and natural history of the Hebridean
islands of Iona and Mull.
Submission Instructions: Sorry, no
unsolicited manuscripts.
Distributor: BookSource,
50 Cambuslang Road
Cambuslang
Glasgow G32 8NB
Tel: 0845 370 0067
Fax: 0845 370 0068
Status of membership: Small Press

NMS ENTERPRISES LIMITED – PUBLISHING

National Museums of Scotland,
Chambers Street,
Edinburgh EH1 1JF
Tel: 0131 247 4026
Fax: 0131 247 4012
E-mail: publishing@nms.ac.uk
Web site: www.nms.ac.uk
ISBNs and imprints:
ISBN 10: 0 948636 Trustees of the
National Museums of Scotland;
1 901633; 1 905267 NMS Enterprises
Limited – Publishing
ISBN 13: 978 1 901633; 978 1
905267 NMS Enterprises Limited –
Publishing
Company established: 1985 as
National Museums of Scotland;
2002 as NMS Enterprises Limited –
Publishing
Titles in print: 60
Contacts: Lesley Taylor
(Publishing Director),
Kate Blackadder
(Marketing and Publicity),
Rajeev Jose (Administrator)
Types of books published: Trade;
scholarly books on: history; art;
archaeology, science; technology;
geology; ethnography; natural history;
popular Scottish history and culture;
biography; photographic archive
Submission instructions: Send an
outline and a covering letter in the first
instance.

Distributor: Scotland: BookSource,
50 Cambuslang Road
Cambuslang
Glasgow G32 8NB
Tel: 0845 370 0067
Fax: 0845 370 0068 UK (except
Scotland) and Europe: Gazelle Book
Services Ltd
USA: Woodstocker Books/Antique
Collectors Club
Orders (toll free) 800 669 9080
Fax: 845 679 4093
E-mail: woodstocker@
woodstockerbooks.com
Canada: Codasat Canada Ltd.,
Suite 1, 4335 West 10th Avenue,
Vancouver, BC V6R 2H6, Canada
Tel: 604 222 2955
Fax: 604 222 2965
Status of membership: Full

PENGUIN SCOTLAND
4 Keith Terrace,
Edinburgh, EH4 3NJ
Tel: 0131 343 6674
Fax: 0131 343 6674
Web site: www.penguin.co.uk
ISBNs and imprints:
ISBN 13: 978 0 141 Penguin;
978 0 241 Hamish Hamilton;
978 0 6709 Viking;
978 0 718 Michael Joseph
Company Established:
2004 (Penguin Scotland);
1935 (Penguin UK)
Contacts: Judy Moir (Editorial); Sarah
Wright (Scottish Sales 078 02 608
806); Anna Ridley, Amelia Fairney
(Publicity 020 7010 3251 or 020 7010
3247)
Types of books published: Fiction
and non-fiction.
Distributor: Pearson Distribution
Services, Edinburgh Gate, Harlow
Essex, CM20 2JE
Status of membership: Full

pocket mountains

PERTH AND KINROSS COUNCIL LIBRARIES AND LIFELONG LEARNING

AK Bell Library,
York Place,
Perth PH2 8EP
Tel: 01738 444949
Fax: 01738 477010
E-mail: library@pkc.gov.uk
Web site: www.pkc.gov.uk/library
ISBNs and imprints:
ISBN 10: 0 905452
ISBN 13: 978 0 905452
Company established: 1988
Titles in print: over 20
Contact: Caroline Beaton
(Community Libraries Manager)
Types of books published:
Books of local interest; local authors;
general.
Distributor: AK Bell Library
Tel: 01738 477 949
Status of membership: Library

POCKET MOUNTAINS LTD

Belstane House
6 Church Wynd
Bo'ness,
West Lothian EH51 OAN
Tel: 01506 500 404/ 402
Fax: 01506 500 405
E-mail: info@pocketmountains.com
Web site:
www.pocketmountains.com
ISBNs and imprints:
ISBN 10: 0 9544217, 0 9550822
ISBN 13: 978 0 9544217,
978 0 9550822
Company established: 2002
Titles in print:12
Contacts: Robbie Porteous,
April Simmons (Directors)
Types of books published: Active
outdoors, including walking, cycling
and wildlife.
Notes on submitting work:
Submissions with return postage
welcome.
Distributor: Cordee,
3a De Montfort Street,
Leicester LE1 7HD
Tel: 0116 254 3579
Fax: 0116 247 1176
E-mail: sales@cordee.co.uk
Also from BookSource, Lomond,
Bookspeed and Nicolson Maps
Status of membership: Full

ROYAL
BOTANIC
GARDEN
EDINBURGH

RCAHMS

ROYAL BOTANIC GARDEN EDINBURGH

20a Inverleith Row,
Edinburgh EH3 5LR
Tel: 0131 552 7171
Fax: 0131 248 2901
E-mail: pps@rbge.org.uk
Web site: www.rbge.org.uk
ISBNs and imprints:
ISBN 10: 1 872291
ISBN 13: 978 1 872291
Company established: RBGE
established 1670, NDPB since 1986.
Titles in print: 38
Contacts: Hamish Adamson
(Publications Manager)
Types of books published:
Botanical, horticultural interest,
scientific.
Status of Membership: Small press

ROYAL COMMISSION ON THE ANCIENT AND HISTORICAL MONUMENTS OF SCOTLAND

John Sinclair House,
16 Bernard Terrace,
Edinburgh EH8 9NX
Tel: 0131 662 1456
Fax: 0131 662 1477
E-mail: info@rcahms.gov.uk
Web site: www.rcahms.gov.uk
ISBNs and imprints:
ISBN 10: 1 902419
ISBN 13: 978 1 902419
Company established: 1908
Titles in print: 34
Contacts: Rebecca M Bailey (Head
of Education and Outreach)
Types of books published:
Illustrated surveys and catalogues
analysing the architecture and
archaeology of Scotland.
Distributor: RCAHMS; Bookspeed
(some titles); RIAS (some titles)
Status of membership: Associate

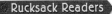

RUCKSACK READERS

Landrick Lodge,
Dunblane FK15 0HY
Tel: 01786 824696
Fax: 01786 825090
E-mail: info@rucsacs.com
Web site: www.rucsacs.com
ISBNs and imprints:
ISBN 10: 1 89848
ISBN 13: 978 1 898481
Company established: 2000
Titles in print: 14
Contact: Jacquetta Megarry
Types of books published: Full colour books with built-in maps for long distance walkers and climbers in rucksack-friendly format on waterproof paper. Classic series includes adventurous walks in Scotland, Ireland and worldwide; new Rucksack Pocket Summits series covers the seven summits of the seven continents.
Submission instructions: Please e-mail with synopsis, sample section and a clear statement of which of our two formats the proposed guidebook would suit.
Distributor: BookSource,
50 Cambuslang Road
Cambuslang
Glasgow G32 8NB
Tel: 0845 370 0067
Fax: 0845 370 0068
Status of membership: Small Press

RUTLAND PRESS, THE

15 Rutland Square,
Edinburgh EH1 2BE
Tel: 0131 229 7545
Fax: 0131 228 2188
E-mail: rutland@rias.org.uk
Web site: www.rias.org.uk
ISBNs and imprints:
ISBN 10: 1 873190; 0 950146
ISBN 13: 978 1 873190
Company established: 1994
(previously RS Publications 1982)
Titles in print: 33
Types of books published: The Illustrated Architectural Guides to Scotland series (currently numbering 22), Architectural Reference and Monographs
Distributor: BookSource,
50 Cambuslang Road
Cambuslang
Glasgow G32 8NB
Tel: 0845 370 0067
Fax: 0845 370 0068
Representation: SEOL
Status of membership: Full

SAINT ANDREW PRESS

121 George Street,
Edinburgh EH2 4YN
Tel: 0131 240 2253
Fax: 0131 220 3113
E-mail: standrewpress@
cofscotland.org.uk
Web site:
www.churchofscotland.org.uk/
standrewpress
ISBNs and imprints:
ISBN 13: 978 0 7152 (Saint Andrew
Press); 978 0 86153 (Church of
Scotland) 978 1 904325 (Scottish
Christian Press)
Company established: 1954
Titles in print: 188
Contacts: Ann Crawford (Head of
Publishing), Richard Allen (Editorial
and Marketing Manager), Christine
Causer (Administrator)
Types of books published: High-
quality titles for the Christian and
general markets. Christian thought
and worship, Scottish interest, history,
biography. Titles with a wide religious
or spiritual appeal that will meet the
needs of readers with enquiring minds
and an interest in thought-provoking
writing. Saint Andrew Press has
merged with Scottish Christian Press
and is now the sole publishing house
of the Church of Scotland.
Distributor: STL,
Saint Andrew Press orders,
PO Box 284, Carlisle CA3 0WZ
Freefone orderline: 0800 28 27 28
Freefax orderline: 0800 28 25 30
E-mail: salesline@stl.org
Web site: www.stl.org
Status of membership: Full

SALTIRE SOCIETY, THE

9 Fountain Close,
22 High Street,
Edinburgh EH1 1TF
Tel: 0131 556 1836
Fax: 0131 557 1675
E-mail: saltire@saltiresociety.org.uk
Web site: www.saltiresociety.org.uk
ISBNs and imprints:
ISBN 10: 0 854110; 0 863340;
0 904265
ISBN 13: 978 0 854110;
978 0 86334 0; 978 0 904265
The Saltire Society
Society established: 1936
Titles in print: 34
Contacts: SEOL Ltd (Marketing,
Sales), West Newington House,
10 Newington Road, Edinburgh
EH9 1QS. Tel: 0131 668 1458; Ian
Scott (Editorial), c/o Saltire Society,
9 Fountain Close, 22 High Street,
Edinburgh EH1 1TF; Paul Scott
(Committee Convener), c/o Saltire
Society, 9 Fountain Close,
22 High Street, Edinburgh EH1 1TF.
Types of books published:
Scottish and Gaelic interest; history;
current affairs; criticism; biography.
Distributor: BookSource,
50 Cambuslang Road
Cambuslang
Glasgow G32 8NB
Tel: 0845 370 0067
Fax: 0845 370 0068
Status of membership: Full

SANDSTONEPRESS
CONTEMPORARY QUALITY READING

SANDSTONE PRESS LTD

PO Box 5725,
1 High Street
Dingwall,
Ross-shire IV15 9WJ
Tel: 01349 862583
Fax: 01349 862583
E-mail: info@sandstonepress.com
Web site: www.sandstonepress.com
ISBNs and imprints:
ISBN 10: 0 9546333
ISBN 13: 978 0 9546333
Company Established: 2002
Contacts: Robert Davidson
(Managing Editor); Moira Forsyth
(Director); Iain Gordon (Company
Secretary); Angus Peter Campbell
(Gaelic Consultant)
Types of books published:
Specialists in the field of Adult Literacy
with the Sandstone Vista Series,
Sandstone Press also publishes
Gaelic fiction to a primarily
educational market, autobiography
and cultural criticism and comment,
and geopoetics.
Distributor: Booksource,
50 Cambuslang Road
Cambuslang
Glasgow G32 8NB
Tel: 0845 370 0067
Fax: 0845 370 0068
Status of membership: Full

SCOTCH MIST PRODUCTIONS

11 Etrick Terrace
Hawick
TD9 9LG
Tel: 01450 370 431
E-mail: postmaster@
darmstrong.demon.co.uk
Contact: Derek Stewart
ISBNs and Imprints:
ISBN 10: 0 954485
ISBN 13: 978 0 954485
Type of Books Published: General
Fiction and non-fiction; humour; local
history.
Submission Instructions: No
unsolicited manuscripts.
Distributor: Scotch Mist Productions
Status of Membership: Small Press

SCOTTISH BOOK TRUST

Sandeman House,
Trunk's Close,
55 High Street,
Edinburgh EH1 1SR
Tel: 0131 524 0160
Fax: 0131 524 0161
E-mail: info@scottishbooktrust.com
Web site:
www.scottishbooktrust.com
ISBNs and imprints:
ISBN 10: 1 901077
ISBN 13: 978 1 901077;
987 1 841801
Company established: 1961
Titles in print: n/a
Contact: Marc Lambert (Chief
Executive); Jeanette Harris (General
Manager); Tessa MacGregor; Caitrin
Armstrong; Philippa Cochrane; Anna
Gibbons; Christian Hasler; Sophie
Moxon; Catriona Scott; Tamara Ogilvie
Types of books published:
Beginning with Books (available in 10
languages), Read Around Books, 'Girl
in Red' by Vicki Feaver, 'Poet's
Polemic' by John Burnside, '100 Best
Scottish Books of All Time' (co-
published with The List and Orange),
'Voyage of Intent' by James
Robertson (co-published by Luath
Press) and 'Scotland 2020: Hopeful
Stories for a Northern Nation' (co-
published with Demos).
Distributors: Glowworm Books,
Units 3 & 4 Bishopgate Business
Park, 189a West Main Street,
Broxburn EH52 5LH
Tel: 01506 857 570
Fax: 01506 858 100
Status of membership: Associate

SCOTTISH NATURAL HERITAGE

Battleby, Redgorton,
Perth PH1 3EW and
17 Rubislaw Terrace,
Aberdeen
AB10 1XE
Tel: 01738 458530/01224 654330
Fax: 01738 827411/01224 630250
E-mail: pam.malcolm@snh.gov.uk
Web site: www.snh.org.uk
ISBNs and imprints:
ISBN 10: 1 85397
Company established: 1992
Titles in print: c.400
Contact: Pam Malcolm
(Publications Officer)
Types of books published:
Environment; natural heritage;
government and education
Submission instructions:
Unsolicited manuscripts are not
accepted.
Distributor: Scottish Natural
Heritage, Battleby, Redgorton, Perth
Tel: 01738 458530
Status of membership: Full

S·C·R·A·N

SCOTTISH TEXT SOCIETY

27 George Square,
Edinburgh EH8 9LD

Please use contact address:
Dr N Royan (Editorial Secretary),
School of English Studies,
University of Nottingham,
University Park, Nottingham NG7 2RD

E-mail: editorialsecretary@
scottishtextsociety.org

Web site:
www.scottishtextsociety.org

ISBNs and imprints:
ISBN 10: 1 897976; 0 9500245
ISBN 13: 978 1 897976

Company established: 1882

Titles in print: 30

Types of books published: Editions
of Scottish texts, chiefly of the
medieval and Renaissance periods
and including works of historiography,
theology and imaginative literature.

Submission instructions: Potential
editors should send an outline of the
proposed edition to the secretary, for
submission to the council.

Distributor: Boydell & Brewer Ltd,
PO Box 9, Woodbridge
Suffolk IP12 3DF
Tel: 01394 610 600
Fax: 01394 610 316

Status of membership: Full

SCRAN (www.scran.ac.uk)

17 Kittle Yards,
Causewayside,
Edinburgh EH9 1PJ

Tel: 0131 662 1211

Fax: 0131 662 1511

E-mail: neil.fraser@scran.ac.uk

Web site: www.scran.ac.uk

Company established: 1995

Titles in print: 33

Contacts: Neil Fraser
(Marketing Officer)

Types of books published: Scran
provides access to the treasures of
Scotland's museums, galleries,
libraries, archives and historic
buildings, on-line and on CD-ROMs,
for education and publishing. It gives
access to thousands of images,
sound clips, movie clips, on-line
articles and journals, and provides an
important networked, multimedia
resource base for the study, teaching
and appreciation of history and
material culture in Scotland.

Distributor: Contact Neil Fraser

Status of membership: Full

sportscotland

SHETLAND TIMES LTD, THE

Gremista, Lerwick,
Shetland ZE1 0EP
Tel: 01595 693622
Fax: 01595 694637
E-mail:
publishing@shetland-times.co.uk
Web site: www.shetland-books.co.uk
ISBNs and imprints:
ISBN 10: 0 900662; 1 904746;
1 898852
ISBN 13: 978 0 900662;
978 1 904746; 978 1 898852
Company established: 1872
Titles in print: 75
Contacts: June Wishart (Managing
Director), Charlotte Black (Publications
Manager)
Types of books published:
Local interest.
Distributor: Mainland Scotland and
Western Isles: BookSource,
50 Cambuslang Road
Cambuslang
Glasgow G32 8NB
Tel: 0845 370 0067
Fax: 0845 370 0068
Elsewhere: The Shetland Times
Bookshop, 71–79 Commercial Street,
Lerwick, Shetland ZE1 0AJ
Tel: 01595 695531
Fax: 01595 692897
Status of membership: Full

SPORTSCOTLAND

Caledonia House,
Redheughs Rigg,
South Gyle,
Edinburgh EH12 9DQ
Tel: 0131 317 7200
Fax: 0131 317 7202
E-mail: library@sportscotland.org.uk
Web site: www.sportscotland.org.uk
ISBNs and imprints:
ISBN 10: 1 85060
ISBN 13: 978 1 85060
Titles in print: c.100
Company established: 1972
(formerly Scottish Sports Council)
Contact: Ken Miller, Head of
Marketing
Types of books published: Sport
strategy documents; sport research;
safety in sport literature and governing
body information.
Distributor: sportscotland
Status of membership: Full

ULSTER HISTORICAL FOUNDATION

Balmoral Buildings,
12 College Square East,
Belfast, BT1 6DD,
Northern Ireland
Tel: 028 9033 2288
Fax: 028 9023 9885
E-mail: enquiry@uhf.org.uk
Web site: www.ancestryireland.com
and www.booksireland.org
ISBNs and imprints:
ISBN 10: 0901905 (older titles);
1903688 (newer titles)
ISBN 13: 978 1 903688 (newer titles)
Company established: 1956
Titles in print: c.150
Contacts: Fintan Mullan (Executive
Director), Kathryn McKelvey (Office
Manager), Marie Heading
(Publications Officer)
Types of books published: Irish
and Ulster history and local history,
genealogy, non-fiction, historical
references and gravestone inscrip-
tions.
Submission instructions: Sample
chapter, synopsis of text, chapter
titles and short description, bibliog-
raphy.
Distributor: Contact Ulster Historical
Foundation
Status of membership: Associate

W GREEN

21 Alva Street,
Edinburgh EH2 4PS
Tel: 0131 225 4879
Fax: 0131 225 2104
E-mail:
wgreen.enquiries@thomson.com
Web site:
www.wgreen.thomson.com
ISBNs and imprints:
ISBN 10: 0 4140
ISBN 13: 978 04140
Contacts: Gilly Grant (Director),
Alan Bett (Marketing Manager)
Types of books published: Law
Distributor: International Thomson
Publishing Services
Status of membership: Full

WEST DUNBARTONSHIRE LIBRARIES AND MUSEUMS

Library HQ,
Levenford House,
Helenslee Road,
Dumbarton G82 4AH
Tel: 01389 608 045
Fax: 01389 608 044
E-mail:
ian.baillie@west-dunbarton.gov.uk
Web site:
www.west-dunbarton.gov.uk
ISBNs and imprints:
ISBN10: 0 9537736
Company established: 1996 (at local government re-organisation)
Titles in print: 17 (originally published by Clydebank District Libraries and Dumbarton District Libraries)
Contacts: Ian Baillie (0141 952 1416)
Types of books published:
Local history.
Distributor: West Dunbartonshire Libraries & Cultural Services.
Status of membership: Library

WHITTLES PUBLISHING

Dunbeath Mains Cottages,
Dunbeath,
Caithness KW6 6EY
Tel: 01593 731333
Fax: 01593 731400
E-mail: info@whittlespublishing.com
Web site:
www.whittlespublishing.com
ISBNs and imprints:
ISBN 10: 1 870325; 1 904445
ISBN 13: 978 1 870325; 978 1 904445
Company established: 1986
Titles in print: 80
Contacts: Dr Keith Whittles (Editorial, Sales), Mrs Sue Steven (Sales and Promotion)
Types of books published: Civil and structural engineering; geomatics; geosciences; nature writing/outdoors; maritime; pharology; military history and selected fiction.
Distributor: BookSource,
50 Cambuslang Road
Cambuslang
Glasgow G32 8NB
Tel: 0845 370 0067
Fax: 0845 370 0068
Status of membership: Full

Non-member publishers

CAULDRON PRESS LTD
Parton House Stables
Castle Douglas
Kirkcudbrightshire
Scotland
DG7 3NB
Tel: 01644 470260
E-mail: allan@lyricalscotland.com
Web site: www.lyricalscotland.com
ISBNs and imprints:
ISBN 10: 0 9536897 Lyrical Scotland
Company established: 1994
Titles in print: 14
Contact: Allan Wright (Creative Director)
Types of book published: Scottish landscape and cityscape monographs; CD-ROM virtual journeys; Scottish view calendars and postcards.
Distributor: BookSource,
50 Cambuslang Road
Cambuslang
Glasgow G32 8NB
Tel: 0845 370 0067
Fax: 0845 370 0068

CLAN BOOKS
Clandon House
The Cross
Doune, Perthshire
FK16 6BE
Tel: 01786 841330
Fax: 01786 841326
E-mail: clanbooks@intertrade1.net
ISBNs and Imprints:
ISBN 10: 1 873597 (Clan Books)
ISBN 13: 978 1 873597 (Clan Books)
Business Established: 1983
Titles in print: 15
Contact: David Warburton (unsolicited manuscripts not accepted).
Type of books published: Guides for walkers in the Scottish countryside.
Distributor: BookSource,
50 Cambuslang Road
Cambuslang
Glasgow G32 8NB
Tel: 0845 370 0067
Fax: 0845 370 0068

COLIN BAXTER PHOTOGRAPHY LTD

The Old Dairy,
Woodlands Industrial Estate,
Grantown-on-Spey,
Moray PH26 3NA
Tel: 01479 873999
Fax: 01479 873888
E-mail: sales@colinbaxter.co.uk
Web site: www.colinbaxter.co.uk
ISBNs and imprints:
ISBN 10: 0 948661; 1 900455;
1 84107
ISBN 13: 978 0 948661;
978 1 900455; 978 1 84107
Company established: 1982
Titles in print: 111
Contacts: Mike Rensner (Editorial,
Production), Colin Baxter (Managing
Director)
Types of books published: High-
quality photographic books on
landscape and natural history; guide-
books; also calendars, postcards,
greetings cards and maps.
Distributor: Colin Baxter
Photography Ltd

FACET PUBLISHING

(formerly Library
Association Publishing)
7 Ridgmount Street,
London WC1E 7AE
Tel: 020 7255 0590
Fax: 020 7255 0591
E-mail: info@facetpublishing.co.uk
Web site: www.facetpublishing.co.uk
Contact: Mark O'Loughlin (Marketing
Manager)
Objectives: Facet Publishing is one
of the leading publishers worldwide in
the specialist field of library and
information science. It has a comprehensive and dynamic list covering all
the major areas of professional activity
and the key skills needed by the
modern information professional.
Description of services: Publisher
of books, training packages, mailing
lists and CD-Roms aimed at library
and information professionals.

HANDSEL PRESS
62 Toll Road,
Kincardine, by Alloa FK10 4QZ
Tel: 01259 730538
E-mail: handsel@dial.pipex.com
Web site: www.handselpress.org.uk
ISBNS and imprints:
ISBN 10: 1 871828
Company established: 1976
Titles in print: 31
Contact: Jock Stein
Types of books published:
Religion, ethics and biography.
Distributor: Turpin Distribution,
Pegasus Drive, Stratton Business
Park, Biggleswade, SG18 8TQ
Tel: 01767 604951
Fax: 01767 601640
E-mail: books@turpin-distribution.com

HARDIE PRESS, THE
17 Harrison Gardens,
Edinburgh EH11 1SE
Tel/Fax: 0131 313 1388
E-mail: admin@hardiepress.co.uk
Web site: www.hardiepress.co.uk
ISBNs and imprints:
ISBN 10: 0 946868
ISBN 13: 978 0 946868;
The Hardie Press; Saltire Music;
Saltire Recordings
Company established: 1986
Titles in print: 30
Contacts: Alastair Hardie, Mary
Hardie
Types of books published: Scottish
traditional music for fiddle, guitar, voice;
Scottish Baroque music; recordings of
Scottish fiddle music, the piano, vocal
and chamber music of Franz Liszt.
Distributor: The Hardie Press

HART & WILL

20 Hydepark Business Centre,
60 Mollinsburn Street,
Glasgow G21 4SF
Tel: 0141 558 0400
Fax: 0141558 4040
E-mail: hartwill@scotsell.com
ISBNs and Imprints:
ISBN 10: 0 9516140
Contacts: Tom Hart, David Will
Types of books published:
Steamers of the Clyde.
Distributor: Direct from the
publishers

LEXISNEXIS BUTTERWORTHS

Scottish Office
Robert Stevenson House
1-3 Baxter's Place
Leith Walk
Edinburgh EH1 3AF
Tel: 0131 524 1784
Fax: 0131 524 1796
E-mail: los.inquiries@lexisnexis.co.uk
Web site: www.lexisnexis.co.uk
ISBNs and imprints:
ISBN 10: 0 406
ISBN 13: 978 1 4057
Contacts: Lucinda Houston
(Service), Eve Moran (Reissue),
John Hogarth (Sales)
Types of books published:
Scots Law
Distributor: LexisNexis Butterworths
Customer Services 020 8662 2000

LOMOND BOOKS

36 West Shore Road,
Edinburgh EH5 1QD
Tel: 0131 551 2261
Fax: 0131 559 2042
E-mail: sales@lomond-books.co.uk
ISBNs and imprints:
ISBN 10: 0 94778; 1 842040
ISBN 13: 978 1 842040
Contact: Duncan Baxter
(Sales Manager), Jackie Brown
Types of books published:
Scottish Interest
Distributor: Lomond Books

MALCOLM CANT PUBLICATIONS

13 Greenbank Row,
Edinburgh EH10 5SY
Tel: 0131 447 6035
ISBNs and imprints:
ISBN 10: 0 9526099;
ISBN 13: 978 0 9526099
Malcolm Cant Publications and
Edinburgh Books
Company established: 1992
Titles in print: 7
Contact: Malcolm Cant
Types of books published: All
aspects of Edinburgh and its environs
including local histories, club histories,
centenary histories etc.
Distributor:
Malcolm Cant Publications

NHS HEALTH SCOTLAND

Woodburn House,
Canaan Lane,
Edinburgh EH10 4SG
Tel: 0131 536 5500
Fax: 0131 536 5501
E-mail:
publications@health.scot.nhs.uk
Web site: www.healthscotland.com
ISBNs and imprints: 1 84485
Contacts: Karen Donnelly (Publishing Manager)
Types of books published:
Health information
Distributor: NHS Health Scotland

RUTHERFORD HOUSE

Scottish Evangelical Research Trust,
Rutherford House,
17 Claremont Park,
Edinburgh EH6 7PJ
Tel: 0131 554 1206
Fax: 0131 555 1002
E-mail: info@rutherfordhouse.org.uk
Web site:
www.rutherfordhouse.org.uk
ISBNs and imprints:
ISBN 10: 0 946068; 1 904429;
ISBN 13: 978 0 946068;
978 1 904429
Company established: 1983
Titles in print: 81
Contacts: Bob Fyall, Lynn Quigley
Types of books published:
Theological doctoral theses, Bible
reading aids and ethical issues.
Distributor: Rutherford House;
mail order

SARABAND (SCOTLAND) LTD

The Arthouse,
752-756 Argyle Street,
Glasgow G3 8UJ
Tel: 0141 221 1900
Fax: 0141 221 7722
E-mail: hermes@saraband.net
Web site: www.saraband.net
ISBNs and imprints:
ISBN 10: 1 887354
ISBN 13: 978 1 887354
Company established: 2000
Titles in print: 18
Contacts: Sara Hunt
Types of books published: Highly illustrated adult non-fiction, specialising in history, the arts, mind/body/spirit.
Submission instructions: No unsolicited manuscripts.

SCOTTISH CHILDREN'S PRESS

Unit 6, Newbattle Abbey Business Park, Newbattle Road,
Dalkeith EH22 3LJ
Tel: 0131 660 4757
Fax: 0131 660 4666
E-mail: info@scottishbooks.com
Web site: www.scottishbooks.com
ISBNs and imprints:
ISBN 10: 1 899827
ISBN 13: 978 1 899827
Company established: 1995
Titles in print: 40
Contacts: Avril Gray (Director), Brian Pugh (Director)
Types of books published: Children's fiction and non-fiction and teachers' resource material written in Scots, Gaelic or English.
Distributor: Scottish Children's Press

SCOTTISH CULTURAL PRESS

Unit 6, Newbattle Abbey Business
Park, Newbattle Road,
Dalkeith EH22 3LJ
Tel: 0131 660 6366
Fax: 0131 660 4666
E-mail: info@scottishbooks.com
Web site: www.scottishbooks.com
ISBNs and imprints:
ISBN 10: 1 898218, 1 84017
ISBN 13: 978 1 898210;
978 1 840170
Company established: 1992
Titles in print: 140
Contacts: Avril Gray (Director);
Brian Pugh (Director)
Types of books published: Scottish
interest books; history; literature;
poetry; Scots language; environmental
and traditional.
Distributor: Scottish Cultural Press

STEVE SAVAGE PUBLISHERS LTD

The Old Truman Brewery,
91 Brick Lane,
London E1 6QL and
6 Hillview,
Edinburgh EH4 2AB
Tel: 020 7770 6083
E-mail: mail@savagepublishers.com
Web site:
www.savagepublishers.com
ISBNs and Imprints:
ISBN 10: 1 904246 (Steve Savage);
0 903065 (Gordon Wright)
ISBN 13:
978 1 904246 (Steve Savage),
978 0 903065 (Gordon Wright)
Company Established: 2001
Titles in print: 34
Contact: Steve Savage (Sample
chapters welcome; unsolicited MSS
not returned).
Types of books published:
Scottish history; language; cooking;
humour; guide books; fiction.
Distributor: BookSource,
50 Cambuslang Road
Cambuslang
Glasgow G32 8NB
Tel: 0845 370 0067
Fax: 0845 370 0068

Scottish Publishers Association Code of Practice

The SPA requires its members to adhere to the following **Code of Practice** in all dealings with their authors.

1. The publishing contract must be clear, unambiguous and compre-hensive, and must be honoured in both the letter and spirit. Matters which particularly need to be defined in the contract include:
(a) a title which identifies the work.
(b) the nature of the rights conferred.
(c) the time scale for delivery of the manuscript and for publication.
(d) the payments, royalties and advances.
(e) the provisions for sub-licensing.
(f) the responsibility for preparing the supporting materials.
(g) the termination and reversion provisions of the contract.

2. The author should retain ownership of the copyright, unless there are good reasons otherwise.

3. The publisher should ensure that an author who is not professionally represented has a proper opportunity for explanation of the terms of the contract and the reasons for each provision.

4. The contract must set out reasonable and precise terms for the reversion of rights.

5. The publisher must give the author a proper opportunity to share in the success of the work.

6. The publisher must handle manuscripts promptly, and keep the author informed of progress.

All manuscripts and synopses received by the publisher, whether solicited or unsolicited, should be acknowledged as soon as received. *Note:* It is important for the publisher to know if the manuscript or synopsis is being simultaneously submitted to any other publisher. In the case of unsolicited manuscripts or synopses, the publisher is under no obligation to give reasons for rejection, and is entitled to ask the author for return postage.

7. The publisher must not cancel a contract without good and proper reason.

Time: If an author fails to deliver a completed manuscript according to the contract or within the contracted period, the publisher may be entitled *inter alia* to a refund of monies advanced.

Standard and Quality: If an author has produced the work in good faith and with proper care, in accordance with the terms of the contract, but the publisher decides not to publish on the grounds of quality, the publisher should not expect to reclaim on cancellation that part of any advance that has already been paid to the author.

Defamation and Illegality: The publisher is under no obligation to publish a work that there is reason to believe is defamatory or otherwise illegal.

Change of Circumstances: A change in the publisher's circumstances or policies is not a sufficient reason for declining to publish a commissioned work without compensation.

Compensation: Depending on the grounds for rejection: the publisher may be liable for further advances due and an additional sum may be agreed to compensate the author, or the author may be liable to repay the advances received. In the former case, the agreement for the compensation may include an obligation on the author to return advances and compensation paid (or part of them) if the work is subsequently placed elsewhere.

8. The contract must set out the anticipated timetable for publication.

9. The publisher should be willing to share precautions against legal risk not arising from carelessness by the author.

10. The publisher should consider assisting the author by funding additional cost involved in preparing the work for publication. If under the contract the author is liable to pay for supporting materials, e.g. for permission to use other copyright material, for the making and use of illustrations and maps, for costs of indexing etc., the publisher may be willing to fund such expenses, to an agreed ceiling, that could reasonably be recovered against any such monies as may subsequently become due to the author.

11. The publisher must ensure that the author receives a regular and clear account of sales made and monies due.

The period during which sales are to be accounted for should be defined in the contract and should be followed, after a period also to be laid down in the contract, by a royalty statement and a remittance of monies due. Accounts should be rendered at least annually. Payment of royalties should be accompanied by a statement of sales and other earnings showing how the royalties have been calculated. The publisher should pay the author on request the appropriate share of any substantial advances received from major sub-licensing agreement by the end of the month following the month of receipt.

12. The publisher must ensure that the author can clearly ascertain how any payments due from sub-licensed agreements will be calculated.

13. The publisher should keep the author informed of important design, promotion, marketing and sub-licensing decisions.

14. The integrity of the author's work should always be protected.

15. The publisher should inform the author clearly about opportunities for amendment of the work in the course of production.

16. It is essential that both the publisher and the author have a clear common understanding of the significance attaching to the option clause in a publishing contract.

17. The publisher should recognise that the remaindering of stock may effectively end the author's expectation of earnings.

Before a title is remaindered, the publisher should inform the author and offer all or part of the stock to the author on the terms expected from the remainder dealer.

18. The publisher should endeavour to keep the author informed of changes in the ownership of the publishing rights and of any changes in the imprint under which a work appears.

19. The publisher should be willing to help the author and the author's estate in the administration of literary affairs.

20. Above all, the publisher must recognise the importance of co-operation with the author in an enterprise in which both are essential. This relationship can be fulfilled only in an atmosphere of confidence, in which authors get the fullest possible credit for their work and achievements.

Copyright

In law, copyright can exist in original literary, dramatic, musical or artistic 'works', and original sound recordings, computer programmes, films, television and sound broadcasts, cable programmes and published editions of works.

As long as the work is original (i.e. not copied wholly or substantially from another work) copyright arises automatically when the work is expressed or recorded in tangible form; there is no requirement for registration or any other formalities to secure protection. The copyright normally rests with the creator of the work who has thereby a number of exclusive rights, which permit him or her to exploit the work in a commercial way. These rights can be transferred in whole or part by assignation or licence, for example, to a publisher.

In the UK, the law of copyright is based on statute, the current legislation being the Copyright, Designs and Patents Act 1988 ('the 1988 Act'). Over the last few years, however, the UK law of copyright has been altered by legal measures emanating from the European Union, the law of which has supremacy over UK law.

Following the implementation of a European Directive, copyright in a work published in the UK during the author's lifetime, now subsists in the work until 70 years from the end of the year of the author's death (previously 50 years). This Directive is applied retrospectively on works that have come into the public domain within the last 20 years. Publishers should seek expert legal advice on titles that were previously out of copyright, and now fall within the 70-year rule.

Protection of copyright overseas remains a high priority for the British publishing industry. While 'piracy' of copyright works is decreasing as more countries sign up to International Copyright Conventions, modern technology makes piracy easy. The moral rights of the author – which is the right of the original creator to have the integrity and source of the work protected – are also acknowledged by the 1988 Act, and may have to be respected by subsequent holders or users of the copyright.

The 1988 Act has attempted to deal with the problem of ownership and copyright within the new technology framework and its associated forms of storage, publishing and retrieval of material. The question of electronic rights remains complex and the increasing use of the Internet makes defence of copyright difficult.

The SPA holds regular seminars on publishing copyright and electronic rights. In addition, a number of books which explain copyright in the UK and abroad are listed in the Bibliography on p.185. Further information may be obtained from:

The British Copyright Council,
Copyright House,
29-33 Berners Street,
London W1T 3AB.
Tel: 01986 788122.

Permissions for photocopying in
academic and educational institutions
are dealt with by The Copyright
Licensing Agency Ltd (see p.105 for
contact details).

Copyright Permissions & Acknowledgements
It is normally the author's or editor's
responsibility to obtain (and pay for)
permission to quote written material
which is still in copyright. Permission
should be sought from the publisher
of the quoted work, not from the
author. In complex cases, such as an
anthology, however, the publisher
often does this work for the author.
Fees for quotation are negotiable and
there is no standard scale.

British copyright law allows free
use of copyright material in two
specific instances – when the material
is used as part of a review or when
used in research or private study. The
sources of all quotations in copyright
(words or music), tables and illustrations should be given, whether or not
it was necessary to obtain permission
for their use. In law, 'sufficient
acknowledgement' means at least the
author (composer, artist and so on)
and title.

Legal Advice in Publishing
The Scottish Publishers Association
can provide advice for its members
on general legal publishing matters.
Specialist legal advice should be
sought from a lawyer. A publishing
law specialist is:

Simon T D Brown
Anderson Strathern WS
1 Rutland Court
Edinburgh EH3 8EY

Tel: 0131 270 7700
Fax: 0131 270 7788
E-mail: simon.brown@
andersonstrathern.co.uk
Web site:
www.andersonstrathen.co.uk

Careers in publishing

Working in publishing can be many things: demanding, a slog, a long haul, exciting, inspiring and challenging … it can also be long hours and low pay, or interesting but hard work for average pay. It could make you a millionaire. But the latter tends to be the exception. Entry into publishing is usually difficult and you should be prepared to accept a job just to get in, and to be flexible and adaptable. Publishing has seen many changes over the last 20 years, so whether you are an editor, or work on very small or very large publicity campaigns or copy-edit for specialist journals, you need to be prepared for some upheaval and change throughout your career. Whichever area of publishing you want to enter you should expect much competition – the Scottish publishing industry has a low staff turnover, and where positions do become available, you will be up against people with experience or who hold publishing qualifications. Experience in related areas, however, is more vital than a holding a publishing specific degree, but most new candidates securing jobs do hold a qualification in publishing.

Work Experience

Once you have decided on which area of publishing you are interested in working, try to gain as much work experience as possible in that area. Remember to be realistic with your initial aspirations; you may be offered work experience in positions other than those you would wish, but this would still be of great benefit in accruing experience. Try to gain work experience in a variety of publishers – small and large, academic and trade – you will then gain insight into how a role can change depending on the size and type of publisher.

Research

Be as proactive as you can. Make sure you research potential employers in detail through their web site, or the *Writers' and Artists' Yearbook*, for example; find out exactly who you should be speaking to and then let them know you are there and willing to do work experience in order to get a foothold. Once in, learn and train so you can move on.

Qualifications and Training

In addition to work experience, you may also want to consider taking some day training courses, or acquire some post-graduate publishing qualification. Organisations such as the SPA or The Publishing Training Centre run short courses in areas such as copyediting, proofreading, design and marketing. Further information about training providers may be found on pp.70-76.

The Society for Editors and Proofreaders is a very useful source of information for those working freelance.

MARKETING:
Fiona Brownlee,
Rights and Marketing Director,
Mainstream Publishing

Fiona Brownlee began her career in books when she joined Pavilion Books, London, as a Publicity Assistant. She is now Rights and Marketing Director at Mainstream Publishing.

I hadn't sold foreign rights until I joined Mainstream in 1997.

My background was publicity but foreign rights is really an extension of PR, the difference being that publishers are a lot easier to deal with than journalists! Over the years several people have sold rights for Mainstream but in the period prior to my arrival no one had had direct responsibility for it. The only people who had attended the Frankfurt Book Fair had been the Joint Managing Directors, Peter MacKenzie and Bill Campbell. Eager to do everything correctly I referred to their appointment schedules from previous years and set up my appointments accordingly. On the first day of the Fair I coasted in at 11am with appointments on the hour blissfully ignorant of the fact that everyone else had been beavering away since 9am with appointments every thirty minutes!

Although they might not have had their schedules packed with formal appointments, Bill and Pete are fabulous at the networking for which Frankfurt is famous. Many deals are struck and contacts made outwith the confines of the Book Fair itself and I found myself hurled in to the social whirl of the bars at the Frankfurter Hof and the Park Hotel. I pity the locals whose bars and restaurants are completely taken over by international publishers but I suppose we experience something similar when the rest of the world decamps to Edinburgh during the Festival. Frankfurt is an extraordinary event. We moan about going but seem to get an adrenaline rush when we get there and survive back-to-back meetings all day and back-to-back parties all night with very little sleep in between. I have made some of my best contacts on the dance floors of post-Fair parties. It is little wonder that I return from Frankfurt each year minus my voice!

Having mastered Frankfurt I realised that there was a whole world out there waiting to be conquered and these trips now include the US Book Fair (BEA) and independent trips to New York. One of my greatest coups was a rights trip around the world, starting in New York and going on to Australia where I visited publishers in Melbourne and Sydney. Although e-mail makes selling rights much easier nothing beats meeting a publisher face to face.

I have now been to nine Frankfurts and eight book fairs in the US. The advantage of being on the

Scottish national stand (set up by the Scottish Publishers Association) means light and space, admin cover for all enquiries in a publisher's absence, and Isle of Arran whisky when things get all too much. The famous SPA whisky party attracts many and the fact that other publishers are on the stand is a bonus. I once sold a book at the SPA party to a publisher who had been invited along by someone else and was strangely drawn to *Saturday Night Forever: The Story of Disco,* which was glistening above my head. My career before Mainstream started when I joined Pavilion Books, London, as a publicity assistant in January 1990. After a short stint at Midas PR working with the likes of Jim Davidson (for Little, Brown), Gloria Hunniford (for Century) and Anthony Hopkins (for Colin Baxter), I returned to Pavilion as Publicity Director in January 1994. In May 1996, I left London to get married and spent a year travelling during which I wrote reports on bookshops around the world for *Publishing News.* In June 1997 I returned to the UK and moved to Edinburgh where I joined Mainstream as Marketing Director with responsibility for the web site and foreign rights. In my first year at Mainstream I was awarded my second award for non-fiction publicity campaign of the year by the PPC, a national award judged by leading agents and journalists. In January 2001 I wrote a feature on my global rights trip for *The Bookseller* and I also reported on BookExpo America for *Publishing News*. I was a member of the Scottish Book Marketing Group until it was disbanded and I am now a member of the SPA Council and am also on the board of the Edinburgh International Book Festival.

FROM EDITORIAL TO PUBLISHER:
Keith Whittles, Managing Director, Whittles Publishing

Keith Whittles began his career in publishing in 1978, moving from academic research into academic publishing with Blackie & Son in Glasgow. In 1986, feeling the need to see publishing from a different perspective, he moved to the Highlands and became a freelance editor, commissioning for several companies. When former authors sought help, and a publishing vehicle, he strayed into publishing under his own imprint. Recent years have seen the creation of technical and trade lists, which are now being expanded.

In 1978 I moved from geological research into academic publishing– with Blackie & Son in Glasgow. Eight and a half years later, and with a desire to do something a little different, I quit Glasgow for the Flow Country.

So in 1986 I did three of the four or five most stressful things a person can undertake – gave up my job, started my own business and moved house. But it was long before the more recent trend for working from home, and it was quite lonely. My decision was met with comments like, 'That's brave of you Keith,' (for which read, 'have you lost your sanity?') and 'You're not taking any authors with you, are you?' I was so green, it never occurred to me.

It took a long time to get established – initially as a freelance commissioning editor and then as a publisher, when authors from my Blackie days began knocking on my door with publishing requests. Then began the routine that so many small publishers go through; dealing with everything, packing books, invoicing, chasing money, *and* trying to generate new titles *and* deal with the promotion of the 'list'.

Then of course something decent comes along, but can you handle it? Not only finding the money to publish it, but what about promotion, etc. Where can I get help? 'Have you heard of the SPA?' says a bright spark. So there, some years ago, began my personal contact with the Scottish publishing establishment, without whose help life would have been distinctly more difficult. The same applies to BookSource – no more packing books on the kitchen table for me.

It is, in some ways, quite a strange existence. I am working with authors all over the world and yet I live in a village of 40 or 50 people, a village that is nearer Stavanger than London, and considerably further north than Moscow. Our office windows looks out upon a wooded valley and from the front door, the Moray Firth provides the backdrop but when I am wearing my reading glasses the view is too blurred to distract me. It can be extremely pleasant, but the travelling costs can be frighteningly large sometimes.

Publishing is undergoing constant change and facing multifarious threats. There is much wrong with the trade and yet so much good publishing is happening. In the shadow of the all-consuming multi-nationals, smaller companies continue to publish some lively, interesting and worthwhile books – of course there is some trash there as well – but perhaps less so on the Scottish scene. Yes, the Scottish scene. It does exist and has a voice that belies its size. I have great faith in Scottish publishing; the people make it so.

PRODUCTION
Catherine Read, Mercat Press

Catherine Read joined Mercat Press in July 2001, after spending a year travelling and working in Australia, New Zealand and South-East Asia. After completing a degree in American Studies from the University of Edinburgh, she decided to stay in the city and pursue a career in publishing. Catherine now works in New Zealand in publishing.

It all went pretty smoothly until I threw away an author's manuscript on my first day at work.

I graduated from Edinburgh University, and after a year of escapism in Australia, decided to apply for my first 'real' job. Not pitching my hopes too high after hearing how hard it was to find work in publishing, I sent off my CV and a few weeks later, I was negotiating my way up a narrow, winding staircase in James Thin Bookshop to my new office at Mercat Press.

Thankfully, I salvaged the manuscript before it was lost for good and managed to avoid any major catastrophes for the next few weeks. In Australia, I'd worked in sales, PR, marketing, accounts and even found work as an extra in an ad campaign. The variety I was accustomed to helped me to settle in at Mercat

Press, as I found that working in a small publishing team demanded versatility. My tasks ranged from editing, typesetting and design to marketing, events and promotions.

However, I'd joined James Thin at a difficult time and within six months of starting my new job, I walked into work to hear the news that the family business was in administration. The subsequent management buyout by Seán Costello and Tom Johnstone was a new beginning for Mercat Press and since then, Mercat has moved to new premises in the West End of Edinburgh, expanded the list, exhibited at the London Book Fair in association with the SPA, set up links with an American distributor, developed a web site and launched a new fiction imprint.

Before I decided on this career, I never knew how demanding and exhausting, but ultimately rewarding the publishing process was. One of the most enjoyable aspects of the job is meeting such a wide variety of people and, for a short time, being part of their dream to see their (sometimes very personal) work in printed form.

Publishing training

Publishing is a continuously developing industry, and, with new developments in print on demand technology, digital publishing, complex design software and updates to proofreading techniques, it is increasingly important for both publishing graduates and long-term staff to enhance and broaden their skills and knowledge.

There is a wide range of courses available for publishers and students, from tailored half-day and one-day seminars and workshops at the SPA (see pp.74-75) to full-time degree programmes at Scotland's Universities. Some training providers also offer in-house courses for companies with specific training needs.

GLASGOW METROPOLITAN COLLEGE

School of Communication and Media,
60 North Hanover Street,
Glasgow G1 2BP
Tel: 0141 566 6222
Fax: 0141 566 6226
E-mail: enquiries@glasgowmet.ac.uk
Web site: www.glasgowmet.ac.uk

The College's School of Communication and Media offers a wide range of courses for those in the publishing industry. They are available at National Certificate, Higher National Certificate (HNC) and Higher National Diploma (HND) level. Many can be studied by either full-time, block release, day release, or evening class attendance.

Courses include Digital Media, Print Media Management, Electronic Publishing, Information & Media Technology, Multimedia, Litho Printing, Fine Bookbinding & Book Repair, Screen Printing, Sales & Marketing, Creative Crafts & Design and Photography.

A course in HND Publishing Studies is now available. Course content includes units in Purchasing & Distribution, commissioning media, publishing & retailing of books, editing and proofreading, niche publishing and preparation for employment.

Further details on courses and how to apply can be obtained from Kenneth Durie, Head of Photography & Printing at the College.

KINGSTON UNIVERSITY

Faculty of Arts and Social Sciences,
Penryhn Road,
Kingston upon Thames,
Surrey KT6 4BW
Tel: 020 8547 8361
Fax: 020 8547 7292
E-mail: hspostgrad-info@
kingston.ac.uk
Web site:
www.kingston.ac.uk/publishing

The MA in Publishing Studies at
Kingston University will prepare
students for a career in the industry,
whether as publisher, agent or
supplier. It will prepare students not
only by encouraging them to acquire
the skills required, but crucially by also
enabling them to understand how
these processes work in a practical
context.

The course is supported by
industry experts at: HarperCollins,
World Book Day, Random House,
Penguin, Serpent's Tail, Kingston
Business School and many more. The
course offers each student work
experience with a publisher. On
completing an MA in Publishing
Studies at Kingston University,
students will be equipped with
editorial, marketing, rights and digital
skills that are in-line with the needs of
the commercial publishing world.

**LONDON COLLEGE OF
COMMUNICATION, SCHOOL
OF PRINTING AND PUBLISHING**

The University of the Arts London,
Elephant and Castle,
London SE1 6SB
Tel: 0207 514 6710
Fax: 0207 514 6772
E-mail: printing@lcc.arts.ac.uk
Web site: www.lcc.arts.ac.uk

Postgraduate certificate (15 weeks),
Diploma (25 weeks) and MA (48
weeks) in i) General Publishing, ii)
Publishing Production. Choice
of two pathways.
Undergraduate certificates: BA in
publishing (3 years full-time),
Foundation degrees (work-based
learning), Printing and Publishing
Production (2 years in full-time – can
gain entry to third year of BA).

LONDON SCHOOL OF PUBLISHING

David Game House,
69 Notting Hill Gate,
London W11 3JS
Tel: 020 7221 3399
Fax: 020 7243 1730
E-mail: lsp@easynet.co.uk
Web site:
www.publishing-school.co.uk

Training institution. Industry-led courses – approved by the NUJ. Trainer for the publishing industry as well as for graduates requiring skills to enter publishing. Short, part-time evening courses and corporate courses can be arranged: Editorial and Proofreading; Magazine Sub-Editing; Feature writing; Picture Research. These courses run for ten weeks, one evening per week from 6.30pm-8.30pm.

Electronic Publishing:

QuarkXpress; InDesign; Photoshop; Dream Weaver; HTML. The Electronic publishing courses run as two-day courses.

NAPIER UNIVERSITY

School of Communication Arts,
Craighouse Campus, Craighouse
Road, Edinburgh EH10 5LG
Tel: 0131 455 6150
Fax: 0131 455 6193
Web site: www.napier.ac.uk/sca
Contact: Caroline Copeland

Full-time, four-year BA Honours degree in Publishing Media. Cognate courses include Journalism and Communication.

One year, full-time postgraduate MSc in Publishing. Entry qualification: an Honours degree in any subject, other than publishing, can also be studied part-time over two or three years.

The School also offers customised in-service courses for publishing houses and related organisations, from copy-editing to new production technology.

OXFORD INTERNATIONAL CENTRE FOR PUBLISHING STUDIES

Oxford Brookes University
Richard Hamilton Building
Headington Campus, Headington Hill,
Oxford OX3 0BP
Tel: 01865 484 957
Fax: 01865 484 952
E-mail: publishing@brookes.ac.uk
Web site: http://ah.brookes.ac.uk/
publishing/index.php

ROBERT GORDON UNIVERSITY, THE

Aberdeen Business School,
Garthdee Road, Aberdeen AB10 7QE
Tel: 01224 263900
Fax: 01224 263939
E-mail:
aberdeen-business-school@rgu.ac.uk
Web site: www.rgu.ac.uk/abs/

Applicants who wish to enter the traditional publishing/bookselling sectors, or the areas of the industry producing serials, magazines or the newer electronic media, may enter the full-time, three-year BA course, the four-year BA (Hons) course in Journalism (only undergraduate 3 and 4 year course is in publishing now), or either of the one-year postgraduate diploma and linked Masters degree programmes in Publishing Studies or in Publishing with Journalism. For staff already employed in the industry, a postgraduate certificate or diploma programme with a linked Masters (MA/MSc) degree in Publishing Studies, Electronic Publishing or Publishing with Journalism is also available by distance learning over one to three years. Areas of study include production processes, marketing, web design, print and broadcast journalism, DTP, specialist publishing, editorial processes, book trade resource management and electronic publishing. Further information from the Secretary at the above address.

SCOTTISH PUBLISHERS ASSOCIATION

Scottish Book Centre,
137 Dundee Street,
Edinburgh EH11 1BG
Tel: 0131 228 6866
Fax: 0131 228 3220
E-mail: katherine.naish@
scottishbooks.org
Web site:
www.scottishbooks.org/training

For the past 20 years the SPA has provided a comprehensive range of training courses, which reflect the needs of an ever-evolving industry. We work closely with our publisher members to design a range of courses suitable for both experienced publishing professionals and those new to the industry. Several new courses are introduced each year; recent inclusions are Guerrilla Marketing and a Print on Demand Workshop.

With carefully selected tutors and consultants, the SPA aims to provide delegates with the latest in knowledge and skills. Courses are held at the Scottish Book Centre in Edinburgh or at The Centre for Publishing Studies at the University of Stirling. We also offer in-house courses and consultancy.

Our programme is divided into three categories:

Publishing Essentials

These full-day core workshops cover the basic technical skills that are required for effective communication and when producing professional publications, such as proofreading, copywriting and computer package proficiency. Publishing Essentials are ideal as skill refresher or introductory courses for delegates with all levels of industry experience. Courses include Grammar Refresher, Proofreading, Copywriting and File Preparation.

Business Skills

Develop your knowledge of key strategy theory in our Business Skills seminars. Each course is led by an industry expert, and will discuss how to make the most effective publishing business decisions possible for optimum organisational development. Courses include E-marketing, the legal framework of publishing and Editorial Project Management.

Industry Seminars

For SPA members only, these exclusive half-day or evening seminars are an opportunity for publishing professionals to discuss the hot issues of the moment, seek advice from industry experts, and learn of the latest industry standards.

In-house Training

For detailed consultancy require-ments, the SPA also offers exclusive in-house training courses that allow organisations to customise the course content to suit specific requirements and systems.

Booking and Information

The SPA training web site is updated frequently and contains an easy online booking facility. Regular e-mail updates are available on request. For the latest brochure, please contact the SPA.

THE PUBLISHING TRAINING CENTRE

Book House,
45 East Hill,
Wandsworth,
London SW18 2QZ
Tel: 020 8874 2718
Fax: 020 8870 8985
E-mail:
publishing.training@bookhouse.co.uk
Web site:
www.train4publishing.co.uk

Courses for people in the publishing industry and for people in organisa-tions that publish, but which wouldn't normally describe themselves as 'publishers'. In-company training and distance learning courses also, covering a broad range of subjects related to publishing.

UNIVERSITY OF STIRLING

The Centre for Publishing Studies,
Room A11,
Pathfoot Building,
University of Stirling,
Stirling FK9 4LA
Tel: 01786 467510
Fax: 01786 466210
E-mail: english@stir.ac.uk
Web site: www.pubstd.stir.ac.uk

One-year postgraduate MLitt course in Publishing Studies, giving an overview of industry structure, varieties of jobs, kinds of editing, production (including word-processing, desktop publishing, electronic and Internet), marketing, legal and financial aspects. Taught through seminars, individual and group projects, and individual dissertation. Staff interests in UK and international publishing. Graduates have mainly found editorial and marketing jobs in Scotland and England; others are in production control, bookselling or related fields. Further information available from the above address.

MASTERS DEGREE IN CREATIVE WRITING

The Edwin Morgan Centre for
Creative Writing
School of English and Scottish
Literature and Language
Faculty of Arts
6 University Gardens
University of Glasgow
Glasgow G12 8QQ
Tel: 0141 330 8538
E-mail: seslladmin@arts.gla.ac.uk
Course Director: Professor Michael Schmidt
Course Administrators:
Lynda Perkins and Wendy Burt

The University of Glasgow offers a Masters course and a PhD in Creative writing. For details of these courses please visit: http://www.arts.gla.ac.uk/SESLL/EngLit/grad/creative.html

Former graduates of the Masters course include Nick Brooks, Anne Donovan, Rodge Glass, Alison Miller, Will Napier, Colette Paul, Rachel Seiffert, and Louise Welsh. Course tutors include Tom Leonard, Janice Galloway, Zoe Strachan, Laura Marney and Alan Bissett.

How to sell more books

Basic toolkit

GETTING YOUR TITLE OUT THERE – BIBLIOGRAPHIC DATA

The following section gives advice on the steps a publisher must take to publish and promote their titles effectively.

How do I get an ISBN and bar code for my book?

Getting an ISBN (International Standard Book Number) for your title is essential as it enables retailers and others to identify and track your book down. Bar codes allow the book's details to be read by electronic means at the point of sale in a bookshop (or at the issue desk in a library). Most bookshops use a system called Electronic Point of Sale (EPOS) which records each transaction and helps to manage the stock orders. Bar codes should be visible on the back cover of each book and can usually be supplied by the repro house or printer, many of which have the software to convert an ISBN into a bar code. If this is not the case you can access a list of bar code suppliers at http://www.aimuk.org/buyersguide.php. At present, the ISBN takes the form of a 10 digit number but that will change on 1st January 2007 when the ISBN will become 13 digits long. More information on ISBNs is available at http: // www.isbn-international.org. Then go to the 'standard revision' section on this web site.

It is not possible to obtain a single ISBN: a block of ten ISBNs is the minimum. The ISBN agency does not issue ISBNs for individual publications. For further information on obtaining ISBNs contact:

The UK ISBN Agency
3rd Floor, Midas House,
62 Goldsworth Road,
Woking,
Surrey GU21 6LQ
Tel: 0870 777 8712
Fax: 0870 777 8714
E-mail: isbn@nielsenbookdata.co.uk
Web site: www.isbn.nielsenbook
data.co.uk

ISBN 13 –
Information for Publishers

The ISBN system for books is changing. After 1st January 2007, all ISBNs will change from 10 to 13 digits in order to extend the capacity of the current system. This change will apply to the ISBNs of both new and old titles.

The ISBN will now include an initial prefix element comprising of a three digit number – 978. ISBNs will retain a check digit, but the calculation method is changing. ISBNs will then become identical to the number of the bar code.

ISBN revision web site:
http://www.collectionscanada.ca/iso/t
c46sc9/2108.htm

All allocations of publisher prefixes under the current ISBN system must be converted to 13 digit ISBNs by the addition of EAN prefix 978 and revised check digit.

The main points you need to know:
• Although the ISBN will change from 10 to 13 digits on January 1st 2007. The bar code does not change.
• All organisations **must** print 13 digit ISBNs on their publications (and any reprints), appearing on or after 1st January 2007. 10 digit ISBNs should not be used after this date.

- In advance of 1st January 2007, the title verso of publications may display both a 10 and equivalent 13 digit ISBN – but **not** just the 13 digit ISBN on its own.
- Publishers must convert all ISBNs in active use as of January 2007 – including backlist titles.
- Old stock does not require stickering or reprinting.
- Publishers may still use ISBNs that they have been allocated, but not assigned to titles. Publishers must convert and exhaust their current ISBN assignment before the UK ISBN agency can issue them with a new allocation.
- Publishers must audit all their ISBN-based systems, old and new, including:
— Contract management
— Bibliographic systems and scheduling
— Purchasing, production management
— Warehouse management
— Sales order processing
— Royalties
— Finance and accounts
— Data warehouse
— Web sites
— ONIX bibliographic files
— EDI files
— Any custom files
— Internal and external systems

Useful web sites

FAQs
http://www.collectionscanada.ca/iso/tc46sc9/isbn.htm

International ISBN agency
http://www.isbn-international.org/

UK ISBN Agency
http://www.isbn.nielsenbookdata.co.uk

Bibliographic Data:
The Easy Way

There are very easy things you can do to help you sell more books. It is up to you, the publisher, to make sure that information on new titles reaches your customer and data aggregators on time. All book buyers work to a strict timetable. If you miss these dates, you will not get sales. You need to ensure, of course, that your data is accurate. Some book chains in the US are now charging for inaccurate data and for the time it takes them to correct this. Good data means better sales because you will reach more markets, have a better-informed sales force, and get your titles listed on bibliographic databases around the world. So even if you may not have a distributor or rights sales in Europe or the US, booksellers and librarians will have access to your books through bibliographic databases.

At present the publishing industry is moving towards using a standard for describing and communicating bibliographic data. This system, called ONIX International (Online Information eXchange), defines the kinds of consistent information that your customers, whether online or not, will require, and specifies how to store and send that information. ONIX is a worldwide standard being adopted Europe, the US, and elsewhere. The advantages of creating your data in the same format as major retailers,

libraries, Amazon, Play.com, Tesco, and others across the world wish to receive it are obvious. For more information on ONIX, go to www.editeur.org.

You need to classify your books into subject genres on the Advanced Information and in bibliographic data and you must look up the Book Industry Communication web site for the standard industry codes, www.bic.org.uk.

Send your AI/bibliographic data out to every data aggregator early

– and make sure your books are listed in most markets/countries to maximise chances of sales. You should aim to send your bibliographic data at least 20 weeks before the book is published.

Eye for detail on bibliographic data

Joe Gonnella, Vice President, Inventory Management/Vendor Relations, of Barnes & Noble, made the following points at a conference held by the US Book Industry Study Group (BISG www.bisg.org), and, with his kind permission, has allowed us to print an extract:

Barnes & Noble's current database contains about 3.5 million active ISBNs of which 2 million are missing from the supply chain in some way, so they cannot be ordered. At the time of this article, Barnes & Noble has $6.5 million in orders for books that are listed as 'out of stock with no due date'. We also have $5 million worth of orders for titles that have passed their publication date, and will need to be cancelled if they aren't produced. Getting a print order from Barnes & Noble is something many publishers aspire to at every book fair – why waste a chance?

30% of Barnes & Noble's active titles are missing a cover scan. Barnes & Noble scans many covers ourselves so that number would be even higher without this work. This obviously has a high cost. 60-70% of titles are missing key ONIX data.

Bookshops want to sell a book, but the publisher has the responsibility of getting the key data on a new book, and the editor should write the AI with the author. A good publisher knows what the store bought in the last year, or in similar titles. Note that commas and spelling do matter a lot. Bibliographic data used to be hidden – out of view on bookseller's databases and microfiche. Now your failures and successes are on view for the world to see through online means. Nielsen Bookdata and Bowker do not have time to correct your typos or to tell you that you mis-spelt an author's name. But it won't impress, and you'll lose a sale… maybe many… It's not a case of sell more books now, but sell some books by completing simple, basic procedures.

Michael Cader (*Publishers Lunch.com* and *PublishersMarket place.com*) adds: 'If a fraction of the time most people spend on getting blurbs, giving sales pitches and gathering sales materials was spent on clearly and consistently expressing basic information about the author and the book, the sales would leap. The concrete payoff is there. It is unglamorous and dull, but it's how we get books to the consumers, grow the marketplace and improve returns.'

Bookshops want to sell a book, but the publisher has the responsibility of getting the key data on a new book, and the editor should write the AI with the author. A good publisher knows what the store bought in the last year, or in similar titles. Note that commas and spelling do matter a lot. Bibliographic data used to be hidden – out of view on bookseller's databases and microfiche. Now your failures and successes are on view for the world to see through online means. Nielsen Bookdata and Bowker do not have time to correct your typos or to tell you that you mis-spelt an author's name.

But it won't impress, and you'll lose a sale, or maybe many… It's not a case of sell more books now, but sell some books by completing simple, basic procedures.

Michael Cader at *Publishers Lunch*, adds: 'If a fraction of the time most people spend on getting blurbs, giving sales pitches and gathering sales materials was spent on clearly and consistently expressing basic information about the author and the book, the sales would leap. The concrete payoff is there. It is unglamorous and dull, but it's how we get books to the consumers, grow the marketplace and improve returns.'

To whom do I send the information?

Agencies
You will need to make both your distributor and sales team aware of the information to successfully sell your book. Then there is a number of agencies who will list your information in a basic form, free, and for more extended, 'richer' information, you will pay a subscription price. One of the main agencies in the UK is called Nielsen Bookdata. You can send the data in paper form and jacket/cover images to:
bibservs.editorial@whitaker.co.uk

UK Library Market

Bibliographic Data Services in Dumfries, Scotland, will also require your information.

Their basic listing is also free, and again, they will require either in paper format or e-mail the same kinds of information as Nielsen BookData. When your titles are published, send a copy to BDS so they can create the book-in-hand record, a record which is more authoritative than one created from an advance information sheet as information on the title can change between acquisition and publication.

Importantly, BDS are also the agency handling CIP Data on behalf of the British Library. The Cataloguing-in-Publication (CIP) Programme alerts libraries and other book buyers to forthcoming titles in advance of publication. A standardised catalogue record for each title is then created to include the author, title, publisher, date of publication, price and ISBN. Name headings are authority controlled. Library of Congress Subject Headings and Dewey Decimal Classification numbers are added to enable subject access. Up to 16 weeks in advance of publication, these CIP records are added to a range of British Library products and services which are available to public, academic and other libraries, and bibliographic information providers and agencies worldwide. Acquisitions librarians routinely use CIP information in order to place advance orders for new titles.

Send AI's before publication to:

Emma McMillan
Bibliographic Data Services Ltd,
Annandale House, The Crichton,
Bankend Road, Dumfries DG1 4TA
Tel: 01387 702251
Fax: 01387 702259
E-mail: info@bibdsl.co.uk

**When your book is published –
Your Legal Requirement**

Publishers in the UK and Ireland have a legal obligation to send one copy of each of their publications to the Legal Deposit Office of the British Library within one month of publication. Publications should be sent to:
Legal Deposit Office,
The British Library,
Boston Spa, Wetherby, West
Yorkshire LS23 7BY
Tel: 01937 546 267 or
Fax: 01937 546 176.

Further copies must also be sent to the Universities of Oxford and Cambridge, the National Library of Scotland, the Library of Trinity College, Dublin and the National Library of Wales.

These can be supplied by sending five copies of every book produced to:
Libraries Copyright Agency
100 Euston Street,
London NW1 2HQ
Tel: 020 7388 5061
Fax: 020 7383 3540
E-mail: publisher.enquiries@cla.ac.uk

Voluntary Electronic Deposits at the British Library

The British Library has launched an initiative for publishers of CD-Roms/ DVDs (for information rather than entertainment) and e-books to deposit with them to ensure the safekeeping and long-term availability of UK electronic publishing. Deposited content will be recorded and preserved within a dedicated digital storage solution.

UK publishers may view a voluntary code of practice for depositing electronic materials online at www.bl.uk/ about/policies/code prac.html. At present this project and code of practice is voluntary, but is pending secondary legislation.

For further information, please contact:
Andrew Davis
Electronic Deposit Manager
The British Library
Boston Spa, Wetherby
West Yorkshire LS23 7BQ
Tel: 01937 546535
E-mail: andrew.davis@bl.uk

GUIDANCE TO PUBLISHERS ON SELLING THROUGH BOOKSFROMSCOTLAND.COM

The site will endeavour to provide a very comprehensive set of titles to be sold. There are specific criteria for titles to be stocked and we reserve the right to refuse to stock any title which we do not think is appropriate for our market.

The general criteria are:
- Books published in Scotland
- Books by Scottish writers
- Books about Scotland

There will be exceptions. For example, there may be a book written by a Scottish author, not published in Scotland, and of marginal interest to customers of the site, as we see it. (This could be a book on physics, or biology, or a school textbook, for example.) Self-published titles will be considered on their own merit.

To be sold through the site, you *must* satisfy two pre-conditions:
1. You must appear on the database which is collated for us by Bibliographical Data Services of Dumfries. They are seeking information on your titles, *at least 16 weeks in advance of publication*.
2. BDS will create records for us for existing titles if you send them a copy of each of the books you would like included.
3. Please send your AI sheets/ catalogues and other information to:

Bibliographic Data Services Limited
Annandale House
The Crichton
Dumfries DG1 4TA
Direct dial: 01387 702257
Switchboard: 01387 702251
Fax: 01387 702259
Web site:
www.bibliographicdata.com/

You must have an account with
Gardners, the wholesalers. Please
contact them to discuss this, if you do
not already have an account set up.
The contract you have with them is
your responsibility and any negotiation
will be with them, **not the site**.

Gardners Books Ltd
1 Whittle Drive
Eastbourne
East Sussex BN23 6QH
Tel: 01323 521555
Fax: 01323 521666
Web site: www.gardners.com

As well as the above two pre-
conditions, we would like to receive
your information. Please send for the
attention of Liam Davison, the Web
Editor, at the address below:

BooksfromScotland.com
137 Dundee Street
Edinburgh EH11 1BG
Tel: 0131 228 6866
Fax: 0131 228 3220
E-mail:
editor@booksfromscotland.com

BASIC INFORMATION TO BOOST YOUR SALES:

Write an AI in good time and make your buyer go wow!

Every book starts with an ISBN,
bibliographic data and an Advanced
Information (AI) Sheet – an essential
selling tool that tells the world your
book is coming. The AI must sell your
document – contain not only the vital
ingredients that Waterstone's,
Blackwell's, Amazon and every
bookshop in the US, and Europe,
need to know about your book (like
the author, title, format, extent, ISBN,
and five key selling points), but also it
must contain quotes and the vital
ingredients that will make your book
sell. The more information you put
into this document, the more
information a buyer has – be it the
bookseller, or the bookbuyer. Every
empty or incorrect field is potentially a
lost sale – and we are not talking
about selling an extra couple of
copies, but to make the book sell at
all, circulating these details in timely
manner is vital for any sales at all. In
the US at present, publishers are
charged by Amazon and Barnes &
Noble for missing information. So the
AI – the vital bibliographic data you
need to sell a book – is the one key
document that should be written by
the person with the passion, vision
and enthusiasm for the book. It is the
commissioning editor who should
write this key document – and

commission a cover – as soon as the book is taken on. You would be amazed at how many publishers do not include a field on who their author is – note that if a customer is buying online, extra detail like this will help sell your book.

203,000 titles were published in the UK last year – more than in the US.

Some wholesalers who sell books into non-traditional book outlets are asking for data just as soon as you can give it – eight months in advance is not too early for the next tourist season, for example. So timely, good data is vital to help wholesalers and booksellers select your title/s and stock them.

The Importance of Targeted Marketing and Good Design
Inga McVicar

The book industry is turbulent. In this continuing time of change we are all trying to succeed in a market driven by the book buyer's demand for value. Traditional booksellers are adapting; non-traditional outlets are increasing. And book buyers want the right book, at the right price, at the right time.

Publishers need to respond to these changes by proactively selling their books, rather than assuming and hoping they will get onto the shelf, onto the web site, into the supermarket … Publishers must convince both industry buyers and bookbuyers that their books are worth time and money.

Publishers must modernise the ways they market to the consumer and how they reach them. They should focus on each book, rather than marketing their own brand.

When promoting to industry buyers, every campaign has the following basic elements:

1. Publisher understanding of USPs (unique selling propositions) and target market – why this book should be bought, who will buy it and how can they be engaged

2. A fantastic jacket

3. A professional AI which is clear and dynamic

4. Proofs/Samplers – often the content is the most effective marketing tool

5. Creative and original sales materials and incentives – for example, e-mail campaigns; sales presenters; relevant gifts to buyers; author dinners

"Consumer Campaigns cost money … I can't afford it."

Traditional, above-the-line marketing (including advertising) does require a healthy budget, but the return will be significant from a considered campaign. Non-traditional, below-the-line marketing – for example, online marketing, off-the-page offers, and PR – all build word-of-mouth and don't necessarily require spend. The basic requirement is an understanding of the target market, and a creative approach to reaching it.

In 2005, Neil Strauss' *The Game*, published by Canongate, was backed by a wide range of promotional campaigns. A dedicated microsite (which attracted over 1.6million hits in one day alone), advertising, presenter key rings, book proofs and media coverage, including *Richard and Judy*, went hand-in-hand with the massive commercial potential of this book. The success of this book is proof of the fact that publishers must exploit every opportunity to reach the target market.

Lithe and focused, independent publishers are at the forefront of developing new avenues through which books can be sold. Sometimes budget is required, other times imaginative planning alone can win sales. Canny presentation means that a market can be made for the individual title from the independent publisher. What is certain is that publishers can no longer afford to assume their book will be found by readers anywhere on those shelves.

Inga McVicar is a freelance sales and marketing project manager, previously Marketing & PR Coordinator for Waterstone's (Scotland, Ireland and NE England) and Marketing Officer for Canongate books Ltd.
Contact: office@ingamcvicar.co.uk
Tel: 07810 540 651

Bookselling

Bookshops

ACHINS BOOKSHOP
Inverkirkaig, Lochinver,
Sutherland IV27 4LR
Tel/fax: 01571 844 262
E-mail: alex@scotbooks.freeuk.com
Web site:
www.scotbooks.freeuk.com
Contact: Alex J Dickson (Partner)
Subject specialisations: Scottish;
hill-walking; natural history
Special services: Mail order, library
and school supply

ARGYLL BOOK CENTRE
Lorne Street, Lochgilphead,
Argyll PA31 8LU
Tel: 01546 603 596
Fax: 01546 600082
E-mail: rona@argyllbooks.demon.co
Contact: Rona McPhail (Manager),
Lydia MacBrayne (Assistant Manager)
Subject specialisations: General,
Scottish interest; children's.

ATKINSON-PRYCE BOOKS
27 High Street, Biggar, ML12 6DA
Tel/fax: 01899 221 225
E-mail: tomes@atkinson-pryce.co.uk
Web site: www.atkinson-pryce.co.uk
Contact: Sue Kekewich
Subject specialisations: Scottish,
children's, general fiction
Special services: Customer order
service, books mailed all over the UK
and worldwide

BALTIC BOOKSHOP, THE
(RODERICK SMITH LTD)
8–10 Cromwell Street,
Stornoway, Isle of Lewis HS1 2DA
Tel: 01851 702 082
Fax: 01851 706 644
E-mail: rsmith@sol.co.uk
Web site: www.balticbookshop.co.uk
Contact: Donald Matheson
Subject specialisations: Scottish;
local interest; fiction; food and drink;
children's.
Special services: Mail order, special
orders, internet bookselling

BARBOUR BOOKS

108 Kaimes Crescent,
Kirknewton, West Lothian, EH27 8AS
Tel: 01506 882 549
Fax: 01506 883 459
Web site:
www.scottishbooksellers.com
E-mail:
colin@scottishbooksellers.com
Contact: Colin Barbour (Partner)
Subject specialisations: Scottish;
all subjects; schools and libraries;
public mail order.
Special services: On-line shop,
dispatched world-wide

BLACKWELL'S

53-59 South Bridge,
Edinburgh EH1 1YS
Tel: 0131 622 8222
Fax: 0131 557 8149
E-mail: edinburgh@blackwell.co.uk
Web site: www.blackwell.co.uk
Contact: Manager
Subject specialisations: Academic;
schools; medical; business; general;
Scottish; children's.
(Smaller branches in Aberdeen,
Dundee, Edinburgh, St Andrews –
see web site for details).

BLAST-OFF BOOKS

103 High Street,
Linlithgow EH49 7EQ
Tel: 01506 844 645
Fax: 01506 844 346
E-mail: blastoff.books@virgin.net
Web site: www.blastoffbooks.co.uk
Contact: Janet Smyth
Subject specialisations: Dedicated
children's and young person's
bookshop.
Special services: Range of
materials for youngsters with specific
learning needs eg dyslexia, autism,
ADHD

BOOKSTORE AND T.I.C., THE

18 High Street, Inverurie,
Aberdeenshire AB51 3XQ
Tel/fax: 01467 625 800
E-mail: bookstore@A.G.T.B..org
Web site:
www.aberdeen-grampian.com
Contact: Mrs Pat Gosling
Subject specialisations: General;
Scottish; walking guides.
Special Services: Book tokens,
mail order, fax/e-mail orders

C & E ROY

Celtic House,
Bowmore, Isle of Islay,
Argyll PA43 7LD
Tel/fax: 01496 810 304
E-mail: info@roysceltichouse.com
Web site: www.roysceltichouse.com
Contact: Colin P Roy (Manager)
Subject specialisations: Celtic;
Scottish; whisky; natural history and
local interest.
Special services: Mail order,
customer orders

CAMPHILL BOOKSHOP

199 North Deeside Road,
Bieldside, Aberdeen AB15 9EN
Tel: 01224 867 611
Contact: Christine Thompson
Subject specialisations:
Anthroposophy; art; childcare &
development, including special needs.
Children's books; cooking; craft;
folklore & mythology; literature &
poetry. Also stock art postcards and
greetings cards.
Special services: Book tokens

CEILIDH PLACE BOOKSHOP, THE

14 West Argyle Street,
Ullapool, Wester Ross IV26 2TY
Tel: 01854 612 245
Fax: 01854 613 773
E-mail: books@theceilidhplace.com
Contact: Avril Moyes (Manager)
Subject specialisations: Scottish
and international literature; poetry;
politics; art; music; history; natural
history; mountaineering; cookery;
biography; travel writing; children's
books; Gaelic; health; general fiction
and general interest sections.
Special services: Mail order,
customer order service

COLONSAY BOOKSHOP

Port Mór, Isle of Colonsay,
Argyll PA61 7YR
Tel/fax: 01951 200 232
E-mail: bookshop@colonsay.org.uk
Web site: www.houseoflochar.com
Contacts: Kevin Byrne (Proprietor),
Georgina Hobhouse (Manager)
Subject specialisations: Scottish
interest, especially the West
Highlands; new and second-hand
books.
Special Services: Booksearch for
second-hand titles

DORNOCH BOOKSHOP, THE

High Street, Dornoch,
Sutherland IV25 3SH
Tel: 01862 810 165
Fax: 01862 810 197
E-mail:
dornochbookshop@hotmail.com
Contact: Mrs L M Bell
Subject specialisations: Golf;
Scottish; Children's; General.

EAST NEUK BOOKS

3-7 Rodger Street,
Anstruther, Fife KY10 3DU
Tel: 01333 310 474
Fax: 01333 313 333
E-mail: eastneukbooks@quista.net
Contact: John Barker
Subject specialisations: Local and
Scottish titles.
Special services: Book search and
book ordering service

FLEET GALLERY

7 & 9 Fleet St,
Gatehouse of Fleet,
Castle Douglas,
Kirkcudbrightshire DG7 2JT
Tel: 01557 814 228
Contact: Alex Hodson
Subject specialisations: Books for
children and young adults.

GOSPEL LITERATURE OUTREACH BOOKSHOP

78 Muir Street,
Motherwell ML1 1BN
Tel: 01698 263 483
Fax: 01698 275 418
E-mail: books@glo-europe.org
Web site:
www.glo-europe.org/bookshop
Contact: Andrew Lacey.
We are Scotland's leading
independent Christian Resource
Centre. We are a registered charity
and the surplus income from the
bookshop is used to promote
Christianity.
Subject specialisations: Wide
range of Christian literature,
resources, music and gifts
Special Services: Rare book
search. Initialling – Bulk orders for
churches and schools – overseas
orders

HENRY HOGG

78 High Street,
Montrose, Angus DD10 8JF
Tel: 01674 672 227
E-mail: henryhogg@btconnect.com
Contacts: Alistair Hogg
(Partner/Buyer), Kate Hogg
Subject specialisations: Scottish;
sport; cookery; children's; reference;
mass-market fiction; horror and
science fiction
Special services: Postal service
(UK), book ordering service

THE IMRAY SHOP

Fort William Road, Fort Augustus,
Inverness-shire, PH32 4BD
Tel: 01320 366724
E-mail: lmray@imray.demon.co.uk
Web site: www.imray.demon.co.uk
Contact: Christine Donnelly
Subject Specialisations: Scottish
history; Scottish novels and
biographies.
Special Services: Mail Order Service

INVERARAY JAIL

Inveraray, Argyll PA32 8TX
Tel: 01499 302 381
Fax: 01499 302 195
E-mail: info@inverarayjail.co.uk
Web site: www.inverarayjail.co.uk
Contact: Mitzi Dando
Subject specialisations: Crime
and punishment
Special services: Postal service,
book search, special orders

IONA COMMUNITY'S SHOP, THE

The Abbey, Isle of Iona,
Argyll PA76 6SN
Tel: 01681 700404
Fax: 01681 700772
E-mail: books@icshop.fsnet.co.uk
Web site: www.iona.org.uk
Subject specialisations: Christian
books and music (especially Wild
Goose Publications); Social Justice;
Celtic; Scottish and poetry.
Special services: Mail order

J & G INNES LTD
107 South Street,
St Andrews KY16 9QW
Tel: 01334 472 174
Fax: 01334 472 174
E-mail: jg.innes@talk21.com
Contacts: Mrs P Innes (Director)
and Miss J A Innes (Manager)
Subject specialisations: General
and children's books
Special Services: Scottish and local
books

JOHN TRAIL LTD
9 Mid Street,
Fraserburgh AB43 9AJ
Tel/fax: 01346 513 307
E-mail: enquiries@johntrails.co.uk
Web site: www.johntrails.co.uk
Contact: Mrs Jennifer J Thomson
(Proprietor)
Subject specialisations: Scottish;
local interest; children's; general
fiction; reference.
Special services: New web site.
Accept credit cards and will mail
anywhere in the world

K MARTIN BOOKSELLERS
14 Main Street, Campbeltown,
Argyll PA28 6AG
Tel: 01586 552 595 and
0141 332 7587 (financial enquiries)
Fax: 0141 353 0263
Contacts: Efric A McNeil,
Iain Wotherspoon
Subject specialisation: General;
children's; Scottish interest

KESLEY'S BOOKSHOP
29 Market Street
Haddington, EH41 3JE
Tel: 01620 826 725
Fax: 01620 826 814
E-mail: sm.kesley@btconnect.com
Web site:
www.kesleysbookshop.co.uk
Contact: Susan or Simon Kesley
Subject specialisation: Fiction;
non-fiction; Scottish history; local
interest; children's; reference; cooking
and gardening; stationary; art
supplies; puzzles and games.
Special services: Coffee Shop/Light
Lunches, New book search service,
school supply, mail-a-book

THE LINLITHGOW BOOKSHOP

48 High Street,
Linlithgow, EH49 7AE
Tel: 01506 845768
Fax: 01506 671811
E-mail: JillPattle@aol.com
Contact: Jill Pattle
Subject Specialisations: Eclectic range of titles, good section of local and Scottish history and a special interest in pre-school age range.
Special Services: Rapid ordering, extra help and advice with early years titles, loyalty schemes in all departments.

LOCH CROISPOL BOOKSHOP & RESTAURANT

17c Balnakeil, Durness,
Sutherland IV27 4PT
Tel: 01971 511 777
E-mail:
lochcroispol@btopenworld.com
Web site: www.scottish-books.net
Contact: Kevin Crowe
Subject specialisations: Scottish interest; poetry, fiction; biography; history; food and drink; gaelic; natural history and environment; children's books.
Special services: Book search service, internet selling

THE MULBERRY BUSH

77 Morningside Road,
Edinburgh EH10 4AY
Tel: 0131 447 5145
Contacts: Peter Reijnierse
Subject specialisation: General; Rudolf Steiner; Education; Child development; Biodynamics; Children's books.
Special Services: UK mail order

OTTAKAR'S

Ottakar's will trade as HMV
Waterstone's from late 2006.

Eleanor Logan (Ottakar's Scottish
Operations and Marketing Manager)
E-mail: eleanor.logan@ottakars.co.uk

Duncan Furness (Ottakar's Scottish
Operations and Range Manager)
E-mail:
duncan.furness@ottakars.co.uk

3-7 Union Bridge,
Trinity Centre, Aberdeen AB11 6BG
Tel: 01224 592 440
Fax: 01224 592 442
E-mail: manager.abd@ottakars.co.uk
Web site: www.ottakars.co.uk
Contact: Vicky Dawson (Manager)
Subject specialisations: Oil and
related industries; children's; Scottish;
academic; business accounts; school
accounts; customer orders.
Costa coffee shop.

87 Grampian Road,
Aviemore PH22 1RH
Tel: 01479 810 797
Fax: 01479 812 274
E-mail: manager.avi@ottakars.co.uk
Web site: www.ottakars.co.uk
Contact: Yvonne Rosie (Manager)
Subject specialisations:
Walking/climbing; Scottish; customer
orders

127-147 High Street,
Ayr KA7 1QR
Tel: 01292 262 600
Fax: 01292 262 150
E-mail: manager.ayr@ottakars.co.uk
Web site: www.ottakars.co.uk
Contact: Alex MacKinnon (Manager)
Subject specialisations: Scottish;
local; customer orders.
Costa coffee shop

79-83 High Street,
Dumfries DG1 2JB
Tel: 01387 254 288
Fax: 01387 257 242
E-mail: manager.duf@ottakars.co.uk
Web site: www.ottakars.co.uk
Contact: Lorraine McLean (Manager)
Subject specialisations: Scottish;
artist materials; stationery; customer
orders

7-8 High Street,
Dundee DD1 1SS
Tel: 01382 223 999
Fax: 01382 202 963
E-mail: manager.dun@ottakars.co.uk
Web site: www.ottakars.co.uk
Contact: Gordon Dow (Manager)
Subject specialisations: Academic;
Scottish/local interest; customer
orders; author events

Plaza Shopping Centre,
East Kilbride, Glasgow G74 1LJ
Tel: 01355 271 835
Fax: 01355 271 840
E-mail: manager.eki@ottakars.co.uk
Web site: www.ottakars.co.uk
Contact: Camilla Wootten (Manager)
Subject specialisation: Children's;
crime fiction; customer orders.
Costa Coffee shop

Cameron Toll Shopping Centre,
6 Lady Road, Edinburgh EH16 5PB
Tel: 0131 666 1866
Fax: 0131 666 1873
E-mail: manager.cto@ottakars.co.uk
Web site: www.ottakars.co.uk
Contact: Fiona Malcolm (Manager)
Subject specialisations: Children's;
local; customer orders

Unit 10-11, St.Giles Centre, Elgin,
Morayshire IV30 1EA
Tel: 01343 547 321
Fax: 01343 545 799
E-mail: manager.elg@ottakars.co.uk
Web site: www.ottakars.co.uk
Contact: Judith Craib (Manager)
Subject specialisations:
Scottish/local; children's; customer
orders

Unit 6, Buchanan Galleries,
Buchanan Street, Glasgow G1 2FF
Tel: 0141 353 1500
Fax: 0141 353 0649
E-mail: manager.gla@ottakars
Web site: www.ottakars.co.uk
Contact: Ian Owens (Manager)
Subject specialisations: Children's
(Launch pad); crime fiction;
Scottish/local; fiction; travel; customer
orders; school accounts; author
events. Costa coffee shop

38 Avenue Centre,
Newton Mearns, Glasgow G77 6EY
Tel: 0141 616 3933
Fax: 0141 616 3255
E-mail: manager.nme@ottakars.co.uk
Web site: www.ottakars.co.uk
Contact: Linda Hartshorne (Manager)
Subject specialisations: Children's;
Scottish/local; customer orders

Unit 69, Eastgate Centre,
Inverness IV2 PP
Tel: 01463 233 500
Fax: 01463 711 474
E-mail: manager.inv@ottakars.co.uk
Web site: www.ottakars.co.uk
Contacts: Brid McKibben (Manager)
Subject specialisations: Children's;
Scottish/local; stationery; academic;
mail order service; customer orders;
school/business accounts; Ordnance
Survey sub-agent. Costa coffee shop

175 High Street, Kirkcaldy,
Fife KY1 1JA
Tel: 01592 263 755
Fax: 01592 263 811
E-mail: manager.kir@ottakars.co.uk
Web site: www.ottakars.co.uk
Contact: Kate Ewings (Manager)
Subject specialisations:
Scottish/local interest; children's;
customer orders

123 George Street,
Oban PA34 5JB
Tel: 01631 571 455
Fax: 01631 571 456
E-mail: manager.oba@ottakars.co.uk
Web site: www.ottakars.co.uk
Contact: Shelly Naughton (Manager)
Subject specialisations:
Scottish/local interest; children's;
customer orders; school accounts

SCOTIA & CHAMELEON BOOKS
17 Register Road,
Kilsyth, Glasgow G65 ODS
Tel: 01236 826 041
Fax: 01236 826 031
E-mail:
info@scotiaandchameleon.com
Web site:
www.scotiaandchameleon.com
Contact: Anna Morrison
Subject specialisations: Specialist
in school and library supplier; support
school curriculum; central warehouse
to shelf buy.
Special services: Exclusive
suppliers of Sapphire Learning – Bags
of Fun

WATERSTONE'S

Kate James: Divisional Marketing Co-ordinator North (Scotland, Ireland, Northern England)
E-mail:
kate.james@waterstones.co.uk

269-271 Union Street,
Aberdeen AB11 6BR
Tel: 01224 210 161
Fax: 01224 211 808
E-mail:
enquiries@aberdeen-langstane.
waterstones.co.uk
Web site: www.waterstones.co.uk
Contacts: Justine Cruddace
(Manager), Iain Dench
(Assistant Manager)

35 Commercial Street,
Dundee DD1 3DG
Tel: 01382 200 322
Fax: 01382 201 730
E-mail:
enquiries@dundee.waterstones.co.uk
Web site: www.waterstones.co.uk
Contacts: Darren Hanna (Manager),
Kitty Ferguson (Assistant Manager).
Café

East End Branch,
13–14 Princes Street,
Edinburgh EH2 2AN
Tel: 0131 556 3034/5
Fax: 0131 557 8572
E-mail: enquiries@edinburgh-eastend.waterstones.co.uk
Web site: www.waterstones.co.uk
Contacts: Colin McGinty (Manager),
Ritchie Hope (Assistant Manager),
Colin Campbell (Assistant Manager)

83 George Street,
Edinburgh EH2 3ES
Tel: 0131 225 3436
Fax: 0131 226 4548
E-mail: enquiries@edinburgh-georgestreet.waterstones.co.uk
Web site: www.waterstones.co.uk
Contact: Neil Johnstone (Manager).
Café

98/99 Ocean Terminal,
Ocean Drive, Leith,
Edinburgh EH6 6JJ
Tel: 0131 554 7723
Fax: 0131 555 4431
E-mail: manager@oceanterminal.
waterstones.co.uk
Web site: www.waterstones.co.uk
Contacts: Robin Crawford
(Manager), Will McLean (Assistant
Manager)

West End Branch,
128 Princes Street,
Edinburgh EH2 4AD
Tel: 0131 226 2666
Fax: 0131 226 4689
E-mail: enquiries@edinburgh-westend.waterstones.co.uk
Web site: www.waterstones.co.uk
Contacts: Ian Webster (Manager),
Megan Campbell (Assistant Manager),
Gillian Duthie (Assistant Manager).
Café

174–176 Argyle Street,
Glasgow G2 8AH
Tel: 0141 248 4814
Fax: 0141 248 4622
E-mail: enquiries@glasgow-argyle.waterstones.co.uk
Web site: www.waterstones.co.uk
Contacts: David McDonald
(Manager), Patrick Douglas-Kellie
(Assistant Manager)

153–157 Sauchiehall Street,
Glasgow G2 3EW
Tel: 0141 332 9105
Fax: 0141 331 0482
E-mail: enquiries@sauchiehallst.waterstones.co.uk
Web site: www.waterstones.co.uk
Contacts: Carol Gardner (Manager);
Iain Johnston (Assistant Manager);
Neil McGaulley (Assistant Manager).
Café

47 Braehead Shopping Centre,
King's Inch Road,
Renfrew G51 4BP
Tel: 0141 885 9333
Fax: 0141 885 9123
E-mail:
enquiries@braehead.waterstones.co.uk
Web site: www.waterstones.co.uk
Contacts: Gordon Alexander
(Manager), Tessa Bowler (Assistant
Manager)

50–52 High Street,
Inverness IV1 1JE
Tel: 01463 717 474
Fax: 01463 714 906
E-mail:
enquiries@inverness.waterstones.co.uk
Web site: www.waterstones.co.uk
Contacts: John Feetenby (Assistant
Manager), Garry Henderson (Assistant
Manager)

St John's Centre, Perth PH1 5UX
Tel: 01738 630 013
Fax: 01738 643 478
E-mail:
enquiries@perth.waterstones.co.uk
Web site: www.waterstones.co.uk
Contacts: Simon Phillips (Manager),
Kath Lydon (Assistant Manager)

Unit 1,
Thistle Marches, Stirling FK8 2DD
Tel: 01786 478 756
Fax: 01786 478 979
E-mail:
enquiries@stirling.waterstones.co.uk
Web site: www.waterstones.co.uk
Contacts: Samantha Leslie
(Manager), Ross MacLachlan
(Assistant Manager)

Organisations

ASSOCIATION FOR SCOTTISH LITERARY STUDIES

c/o Department of Scottish History,
University of Glasgow,
9 University Gardens,
Glasgow G12 8QH
Tel: 0141 330 5309
E-mail: office@asls.org.uk
Web site: www.asls.org.uk
Contact: Duncan Jones

The Association for Scottish Literary Studies (ASLS) exists to promote the study, teaching and writing of Scottish literature and to further the study of the languages of Scotland. Founded in 1970 it is now an international organisation with members in more than 20 countries. ASLS believes that Scotland has a culture and identity that is diverse and highly distinctive and therefore strives to nourish Scottish writing and modes of expression. It seeks to encourage membership amongst teachers, academics, libraries and institutions and general readers. ASLS publishes annually: an edited text of Scottish literature which deserves to be presented afresh to a contemporary audience; an anthology of new writing in Scots, Gaelic and English; a series of literary and linguistic journals; and a twice-yearly newsletter. The Association also publishes *Scotnotes* – comprehensive study guides to major Scottish writers and literary texts for students at all levels, and a series of Occasional Papers – essays and monographs on the literature and languages of Scotland. ASLS organises an annual conference in association with the Annual General Meeting, a Schools Conference held in Glasgow every October and a yearly conference on a language topic.

ASLS membership is open to all. In 2006, a subscription of £38.00 (individuals) or £67.00 (corporate) buys: one Annual Volume, New Writing Scotland 24; Scottish Studies Review (two issues); ScotLit (two issues); Scottish Language (one issue). Special packages for schools and students are also available.

ASSOCIATION OF AUTHORS' AGENTS

c/o Johnson and Alcock,
Clerkenwell House,
45-47 Clerkenwell Green,
London EC1R 0HT
Tel: 0207 251 0125
Fax: 0207 251 2172
E-mail: aaa@johnsonandalcock.co.uk
Web site: www.agentsassoc.co.uk
Contact: Anna Power (Secretary)
Objectives: To provide a forum for member agents to discuss industry matters, to uphold a code of good practice and to represent the interests of authors and agents. Membership is only open to literary agents who have been in business for a minimum of three years and have maintained a level of commission of at least £25,000.

BOOKSELLERS ASSOCIATION OF THE UNITED KINGDOM AND IRELAND LTD

Minster House,
272 Vauxhall Bridge Road,
London SW1V 1BA
Tel: 020 7802 0802
Fax: 020 7802 0803
E-mail: mail@booksellers.org.uk
Web site: www.booksellers.org.uk
Contact: Meryl Halls (Head of Membership Services)
Objectives: Trade association representing 95% of new booksellers in the UK and Ireland. Promotes bookselling through lobbying, campaigning and provision of events, and access to a range of services and products.
Description of services: Lobbying and representation; information; essential trade publications (Directory of UK & Irish Book Publishers and Directory of Booksellers Association Members); annual conference, special events and seminars; professional services and products; Christmas Book catalogue; Book Tokens; batch.co.uk.

BRITISH COUNCIL

Knowledge and Information Services,
Bridgewater House,
58 Whitworth Street,
Manchester M1 6BB
Tel: 0161 957 7182
Fax: 0161 957 7168
E-mail:
publishing.enquiries@britishcouncil.org
Web site: www.britishcouncil.org
Contact: Information Society Project
Officer
Objectives: The British Council is the
United Kingdom's international organisation for educational opportunities
and cultural relations. Our purpose is
to build mutually beneficial relation-
ships between people in the UK and
other countries and to increase
appreciation of the UK's creative ideas
and achievements.
Description of services: 1. Provide
high-quality presence at a selection of
international book fairs and
exhibitions. 2. To provide information
on overseas book markets to UK
publishers and booksellers. 3. To
support the development of
commercial links between overseas
and UK book industries.

CILIPS

(formerly Scottish Library Association)
Chartered Institute of Library and
Information Professionals in Scotland,
1st Floor Building C, Brandon Gate,
Leechlee Road, Hamilton ML3 6AU
Tel: 01698 458 888
Fax: 01698 283 170
E-mail: cilips@slainte.org.uk
Web site: www.slainte.org.uk
ISBNs and imprints: 0 900649
Company established: 2002
Contact: Elaine Fulton BA, MCLIP
(Director), Rhona Arthur (Assistant
Director), Alan Reid (Honorary
Publications Officer), c/o Midlothian
Libraries, Library HQ, 2 Clerk Street,
Loanhead, Midlothian EH20 9DR
Tel: 0131 271 3980
Fax: 0131 440 4635
Services offered: Promotion of
libraries and librarianship
What is CILIPS? The Chartered
Institute of Library and Information
Professionals in Scotland (CILIPS)
was formed in 2002 by the amalga-
mation of the Library Association and
the Institute of Information Scientists.

CILIPS works on behalf of Scottish
members to improve and support
Scottish library and information
services. CILIPs works closely with the
Scottish Library and Information
Council, the advisory body for Scottish
ministers on library and information
matters in Scotland, and shares
staffing, accommodation and
co-operates on many joint projects.

What does it do?

- Represents library/information service interests at national and local level
- Develops and promote standards
- Advises individual members
- Organises an Annual Conference and a Continuing Educational Development Programme
- Publishes a bi-monthly journal *Scottish Libraries and publications* of professional interest

Publications: CILIPS has a small publications programme including the directory *Scottish Library and Information Resources*. The journal is published to keep members up to date with new developments in the professional. The SLAINTE web site (www.slainte.org.uk) supplements and extends that service. CILIPS also publishes some material of Scottish interest.

How is it funded? CILIPs derives its funding from members' subscriptions and from income generated from the sale of publications, conferences and short courses.

COMHAIRLE NAN LEABHRAICHEAN/ THE GAELIC BOOKS COUNCIL

22 Mansfield Street,
Glasgow G11 5QP
Tel: 0141 337 6211
Fax: 0141 341 0515
E-mail: brath@gaelicbooks.net
Web site: www.gaelicbooks.net
Contact: Ian MacDonald (Director)

Established in 1968 within the department of Celtic Studies at Glasgow University, the Council became a separate organisation in its own right in 1996. It is a charitable company, and its purpose is to assist and stimulate Gaelic publishing. It has nine members drawn from various relevant areas of interest, an assessor from the Scottish Arts Council and a paid staff of four. The Scottish Arts Council has been its main funding body since 1983.

The Council provides financial assistance in the form of publication grants (paid to the publisher) for individual Gaelic books submitted by the publisher before publication. It also operates a scheme of commission grants for books as yet unwritten. For these, the author or publisher can approach the Council with a project, or vice-versa.

The Council has its own bookshop in Glasgow, and provides a mail order service in the UK and beyond, as well as sales at special events such as Mods, weekend courses, conferences and other gatherings. It stocks all Gaelic and Gaelic-related books in print, and these are listed in its catalogue, *Leabhraichean Gàidhlig*. The web site also has details of all titles in stock. An editorial service is also available, and the Council regularly word-processes and prepares texts for the press. More details of its work may be obtained from its free Annual Reports.

COPYRIGHT LICENSING AGENCY LTD, THE

CBC House,
24 Canning Street,
Edinburgh EH3 8EG
Tel: 0131 272 2711
Fax: 0131 272 2811
E-mail: clascotland@cla.co.uk
Web site: www.cla.co.uk
Contact: Jim MacNeilage,
Saffron House, 6-10 Kirby Street,
London EC1N 8TS
Tel: 020 7400 3100
Fax: 020 7400 3101
E-mail: cla@cla.co.uk
Web site: www.cla.co.uk
Contact: Peter Shepherd (Chief Executive & Company Secretary), Siobhan Sherry (PR and Marketing Officer)
Objectives: The Agency was formed in 1982 by the Authors' Licensing & Collecting Society and the Publishers Licensing Society, as a single source for the authorisation of copying and to establish and manage licensing schemes for institutional and profes-sional organisations where extensive photocopying of books, journals and periodicals occurs. The CLA has an agency agreement with the Design and Artists' Copyright Society (DACS) for the photocopying of artistic works.
Description of services: The issuing and administration of copying licences and the distribution of the copying fees (via their respective societies) to those British and foreign

authors and publishers whose works have been copied. The CLA has and is introducing a range of digital licences across the education, government and business sectors.

EDINBURGH INTERNATIONAL BOOK FESTIVAL

5a Charlotte Square,
Edinburgh, EH2 4DR
Tel: 0131 226 5335
Fax: 0131 228 4333
E-mail: admin@edbookfest.co.uk
Web site: www.edbookfest.co.uk
Company established: 1982
Contact: Catherine Lockerbie (Director)
Date of 2007 Book Festival:
11–27 August

The Edinburgh International Book Festival is the largest and most successful event of its kind in the world. It is a living celebration of the written word which has been hosting its own unique range of author events, under canvas, at the heart of Scotland's capital city for 22 years. For two and a half weeks it throws a spotlight on national and international literature at a time when Edinburgh becomes a 'Festival City', one of the key cultural capitals of the world.

From 11–27 August 2007, the tented village which houses the Festival will spring up in Charlotte Square, including book shops, theatres, a children's activity tent, a Mongolian yurt, bars and signing tents. All of these spaces provide a fabulous setting for over 600 events, including nationally and internationally renowned authors, the hottest new writing talents and some unexpected literary surprises. They also provide a temporary home for writers, publishers, readers and book enthusiasts of all ages as well as the simply curious. With author conversations, debates, readings, workshops, music and children's events in abundance, the Festival aims to increase public awareness of books and writing and the pleasure and value of reading.

The children's programme is a series of stimulating family and school events embracing story-telling, workshops, readings and talks by authors and illustrators. In this way, children have their first memorable experiences of meeting their favourite authors face-to-face. Children's authors have included Philip Pullman, Jacqueline Wilson, David Almond, Debi Gliori, Eoin Colfer and many more.

Similarly the adult programme brings together writers and their readers as well as introducing new or unfamiliar authors to highly receptive audiences. Writers who appeared at the 2005 Book Festival included John Irving, Salman Rushdie, Margaret Atwood and over 600 more.

Nearly 220,000 people came to the Festival in 2005 and book sales reached a new record high.

EDINBURGH UNESCO CITY OF LITERATURE

5a Charlotte Square
Edinburgh EH2 4DR
Tel: 0131 718 5663
E-mail:
edinburgh@cityofliterature.com
Web site: www.cityofliterature.com
Contact: Anna Burkey (Administrator)

In October 2004 Edinburgh became the first UNESCO City of Literature in the world. The designation serves as global recognition of Edinburgh's rich literary heritage, thriving contemporary scene and bold aspirations for the future. The permanent award has concentrated efforts to attract new literary initiatives to Scotland while enabling the development with future international cities of literature, to establish a worldwide network. To read more about why Edinburgh is the first UNESCO City of Literature, or learn about forthcoming literary initiatives and book events, visit www.cityofliterature.com for the full story, or e-mail us with questions or comments.

FEDERATION OF CHILDREN'S BOOK GROUPS

c/o Martin and Sinéad Kromer,
2 Bridge Wood View, Horsforth,
Leeds, West Yorkshire LS18 5PE
E-mail: info@fcbg.org.uk
Web site: www.fcbg.org.uk
Objectives: A voluntary organisation
for parents, teachers, librarians,
booksellers, publishers and all who
are interested in books and children
from 0-16 years.

Description of services: Local
groups fit local circumstances:
activities range from talks, book sales,
Family Reading Groups and story
times to sponsored author visits and
out-of-school fun events. National
events include National Share-a-Story
Month and annual conferences.
Booklists are published regularly and
include Pick of the Year – 50 top titles
tested and chosen by children and
families for the Red House Children's
Book Award.

BIBLIOGRAPHIC DATA:

Details for Nielsen BookData follow,
but more general advice on
bibliographic data can be found on
pp.77–81, and ISBN 13 on pp.78-9.

NIELSEN BOOKDATA

3rd Floor, Midas House,
62 Goldsworth Road, Woking,
Surrey GU21 6LQ
Tel: 0870 777 8710
Fax: 0870 777 8711
E-mail:
sales@nielsenbookdata.co.uk
Web site:
www.nielsenbookdata.co.uk
Contacts: Vesna Nall (Publisher Subscription Manager), Peter Mathews (Publisher Services Director), Simon Skinner (UK Sales Director)
Description: Nielsen BookData was formed in 2002, following the merger of Book Data, Whittaker Information Services and First Edition.
Contact for Information:
Mo Siewcharran (Head of Marketing)
Objectives: To provide booksellers & libraries with the most up-to-date, timely, accurate and Content-rich book information for all English-language books (and other published media, including e-books), published internationally. The company therefore works closely with publishers and other data suppliers to collect, aggregate and disseminate book information worldwide.
Description: The database has over 6 million unique, up-to-date records giving enriched data with descriptive text, ToCs, subject classifications, literary awards, promotional information and territorial rights. The data is available in a variety of formats: data feed, dynamic XML, CD-ROMs and online services.

Enhanced data service:

Ms Vesna Nall
E-mail: publisher.services@
nielsenbookdata.co.uk

Nielsen BookData – Editorial

Publisher Helpdesk,
3rd Floor, Midas House,
62 Goldsworth Road, Woking,
Surrey GU21 6LQ
Tel: 0845 450 0016
Fax: 0870 777 8711

Publisher Help Desk
E-mail:
pubhelp@nielsenbookdata.co.uk
Publisher Helpdesk handles general enquiries.

Trade Data

All queries relating to price, availability, TeleOrder routing and distribution should be directed to the Trade Data Team
E-mail:
tradedata@nielsenbookdata.co.uk.

New title submissions should be sent to:

Data Preparation, Nielsen BookData, 89-95 Queensway, Stevenage, Herts SG1 1EA
E-mail:
newtitles@nielsenbookdata.co.uk

If you want to change an image:
on Amazon and originally supplied
your data through Nielsen, you must
send your new image to:
images@nielsenbookdata.co.uk
and explain it is a re-supply. It will take
a minimum of 10-20 days to update.

BookNet
(BookData's transaction services)

Objectives: To provide e-commerce
to the industry that delivers a means
of efficient and cost effective trading
between partners regardless of size or
location.
Description: BookNet provides a
range of e-commerce services that
allow electronic trading between
booksellers, publisher/distributors,
libraries and other suppliers. Services
include BookNet Web for booksellers
& publishers/distributors, TeleOrdering
and EDI messaging.
Contact: 3rd Floor,
Midas House,
62 Goldsworth Road,
Woking GU21 6LQ
Tel: 0870 777 8710
Fax: 0870 777 8711
E-mail: sales@nielsenbookdata.co.uk
Web site: www.nielsenbooknet.co.uk

Nielsen BookScan

Objective: To provide online,
actionable, business critical sales
information to the industry.
Description: BookScan collects
transactional data at the point of sale
from tills and despatch systems of all
the major book retailers in the UK,
Ireland, US, Australia and South
Africa. Each week data is coded and
analysed, producing complete market
information for retailers, publishers,
libraries, agents and the media within
72 hours.
Contacts: 3rd Floor,
Midas House, 62 Goldsworth Road,
Woking GU21 6LQ
Tel: 01483 712 222
Fax: 01483 712 220
E-mail: info@nielsenbookscan.co.uk
Web site:
www.nielsenbookscan.co.uk

UK REGISTRATION AGENCIES OPERATED BY NIELSEN BOOKDATA

ISBN, SAN & DOI

Objectives: Nielsen BookData Registration Services provide UK and other English-language publishers with a range of standard identifiers for use in the international supply chain.

Description of services: ISBN Agency issues ISBNs to publishers based in the UK and the Republic of Ireland (can provide help and advice on changing from 10 to 13 digits).

SAN Agency is administered on behalf of the Book Industry Communication. It assigns Standard Address Numbers and Global Location Numbers for organisations in any country except USA, Canada, Australia and New Zealand.

DOI Agency provides web-based registration and maintenance facilities for DOIs and their metadata for use by any publisher regardless of their location.

Contacts: 3rd Floor, Midas House, 62 Goldsworth Road, Woking GU21 6LQ
Tel: 0870 777 8712
Fax: 0870 777 8714
E-mail: isbn@nielsenbookdata.co.uk, san@nielsenbookdata.co.uk
doi@nielsenbookdata.co.uk
Web site: www.isbn.nielsen-bookdata.co.uk
www.sanagency.co.uk
www.doi.nielsenbookdata.co.uk

PLAYWRIGHTS' STUDIO, SCOTLAND

Playwrights' Studio, Scotland
CCA, 350 Sauchiehall Street
Glasgow G2 3JD
Tel: 0141 332 4403
Fax: 0141 332 6352
Web site:
www.playwrightsstudio.co.uk

Originally dreamed up by playwrights Tom McGrath, and following extensive research by Faith Liddell, the Scottish Arts Council awarded funding to create the Playwrights' Studio in 2004.

Led by Creative Director Julie Ellen and an annually appointed team of Associate Playwrights, this year David Greig, Liz Lochhead and Nicola McCartney, the Playwrights' Studio is a national arts organisation designed to celebrate, promote and develop Scotland's rich and growing culture of writing for live performance. It aims to secure a future for playwrights and their work by improving and sustaining artistic quality, raising awareness, and increasing opportunities and access.

Away from the pressures of a producing theatre, the Playwrights Studio will place playwrights at the heart of script development, tailoring their professional development to their individual needs.

PUBLIC LENDING RIGHT

Richard House, Sorbonne Close,
Stockton-on-Tees TS17 6DA
Tel: 01642 604699
Fax: 01642 615 641
E-mail: authorservices@plr.uk.com
Web site: www.plr.uk.com
Contact: Susan Ridge, PA to
the Registrar
Objectives: The Public Lending
Right legislation gives authors a
statutory right to receive payment for
the free lending of their books from
public libraries throughout the UK.
PLR is administered by the Registrar
and his staff whose function is to
collect loans data and make
payments to authors on the basis of
how often their books are borrowed.
PLR is funded by the Department for
Culture, Media and Sport.
Description of services: Register
applications from authors, make
annual payments on the basis of
loans data collected from a sample of
public libraries in the UK. Provide
information on trends in public
borrowing. Produce annual reports
and other publications.

PUBLISHERS ASSOCIATION, THE

29b Montague Street,
London WC1B 5BW
Tel: 020 7691 9191
Fax: 020 7691 9199
E-mail: mail@publishers.org.uk
Web site: www.publishers.org.uk
Contact: Rob Hamadi (Head of
Communications)
Objectives: The Publishers
Association is the leading trade
organisation serving book, journal and
electronic publishers in the UK. It
brings publishers together to discuss
the main issues facing the industry
and to define the practical policies
that will take the industry forward. The
aim of the Publishers Association is to
serve and promote by all lawful
means the interest of book, journal
and electronic publishers and to
protect those interests.

SCHOOL LIBRARY ASSOCIATION IN SCOTLAND

Convenor: Fiona Devoy
Tel: 01324 628 416
Secretary: Rebecca Christine
Tel: 0131 347 5740
E-Mail: schristiner@esmgc.com
Description of services: The School Library Association in Scotland is a branch of the School Library Association which supports all those committed to the promotion and development of school libraries and information literacy. The School Library Association in Scotland usually holds two training days per year.

SCOTTISH CENTRE FOR THE BOOK

SCOB, Napier University, Craighouse Campus, Edinburgh, EH10 5LG.
Tel: 0131 455 6171
Fax: 0131 455 6306
E-mail: scob@napier.ac.uk
Web site: www.scob.org.uk
Contact: Alistair McCleery
Objectives: The Scottish Centre for the Book acts as a focus for research into and scholarship in print culture and the sociology of texts. It hosts seminars and conferences and issues publications relating to the past, present and future of the printed word, its creation, diffusion and reception. It organises the Edward Clark seminars; it publishes *The Bibliotheck*, a journal of Scottish book history and bibliography; and it jointly hosts the SAPPHIRE initiative.

SCOTTISH ARTS COUNCIL

12 Manor Place, Edinburgh EH3 7DD
Tel: 0131 226 6051
Helpdesk Tel: 0845 603 6000 (local rate)
Fax: 0131 225 9833
E-mail:
help.desk@scottisharts.org.uk
Web site: www.scottisharts.org.uk
Office hours: Mon–Fri 9am–5pm
Date established: 1967 as Scottish Arts Council
Contacts: Graham Berry (Chief Executive); Jim Tough (Director of Arts); Morag Arnot (Director of Planning and Communications); Liz Sams (Director of Funding and Resources); Moira Gibson (Head of External Relations); Dr Helen Bennett (Head of Crafts); Anita Clark (Head of Dance); David Taylor (Head of Drama); Dr Gavin Wallace (Head of Literature); Ian Smith (Head of Music); Amanda Catto (Head of Visual Arts); Iain Munro (Head of Capital Lottery); Joan Parr (Head of Education); Caroline Docherty (Head of Planning and Research)
Objectives: The Scottish Arts Council champions the arts for Scotland. Its main aims are to increase participation in the arts; to support artists to fulfil their creative and business potential; and to place arts, culture and creativity at the heart of learning.

Activities: The Scottish Arts Council invests £60 million from Scottish Executive and National Lottery funding to support and develop artistic excellence and creativity throughout Scotland. It supports five national companies: Scottish Opera, Scottish Ballet, the Royal Scottish National Orchestra, the Scottish Chamber Orchestra and the National Theatre of Scotland. In addition it core funds over 100 arts organisations throughout Scotland, sustaining a network of arts companies and centres which provide opportunities for professional excellence and development while offering the means of wider access and participation by the general public.

The Council funds awards, bursaries, fellowships and training opportunities for individuals, as well as for a range of arts projects. Lottery funding prioritises broadening audiences, work for and by children and young people, arts touring to ensure geographical spread, and professional development for individual artists and arts organisations.

Information: The Scottish Arts Council offers a help desk advice service on the arts and arts funding. It publishes reports, guides and research, as well as regular bulletins about its work. Most are downloadable from their web site.

Literature: The Literature Department at the Scottish Arts Council funds a range of literary organisations including the Scottish Publishers Association, the Scottish Book Trust, the Scottish Poetry Library and the Scottish Storytelling Forum. It also supports the Edinburgh International Book Festival, funds a range of work in Scots and Gaelic, and subsidises the publication of a number of literary magazines in Scotland, as well as offering grants to writers, publishers and literary events. In addition, lottery funding from the Scottish Arts Council has enabled the construction of buildings such as the Scottish Poetry Library and the Scottish Storytelling Centre.

SCOTTISH ASSOCIATION OF PROVIDERS OF EDUCATIONAL RESOURCES (SAPER)
38e, Graham Street, Johnstone, Renfrewshire PA5 8QY
Tel/fax: 01505 342 551
E-mail: drew.stuart@ntlworld.com
Web site: www.saper.org.uk
Contact: Drew Stuart (Honorary Secretary)
Objectives: To give expression to opinion of members and to encourage a professional approach to the promotion of texts and materials in educational establishments throughout Scotland.
Description of services: SAPER provides a regular circular of information and requests for display materials to educational representatives of nearly all major publishers and education equipment suppliers: items for inclusion can be sent to the Honorary Secretary (at the above address) from whom details of SAPER's regular diet of Scottish educational exhibitions are also available.

SCOTTISH BOOK TRUST

Scottish Book Centre, Sandeman House, Trunk's Close, 55 High Street, Edinburgh EH1 1SR
Tel: 0131 524 0160
Fax: 0131 524 0161
E-mail: info@scottishbooktrust.com
Web site:
www.scottishbooktrust.com
Contact: Marc Lambert (Chief Executive); Jeanette Harris (General Manager); Tessa MacGregor; Caitrin Armstrong; Philippa Cochrane; Anna Gibbons; Christian Hasler; Sophie Moxon; Catriona Scott; Pam Wardell; Tamara Ogilvie

Description of services: Scottish Book Trust is Scotland's national agency for readers and writers. SBT exists to bring books and people together by providing key services to readers, writers and the educational sector.

We provide:
- Independent advice and information for readers and writers
- Support for literacy and access to book related opportunities for all
- Support for writers and the development of writing in Scotland
- Quality resources to the educational and library sector
- National readership development programmes
- Targeted educational programmes
- National author tours and events

Our key programmes are:
- Live Literature Scotland
- Words@Work
- Reading Rich
- Scottish Friendly National Words on Wheels Touring Programme
- BRAW (books, reading and writing), the network for the Scottish Children's book, was set up in 2005 to promote the work of children's authors and illustrators working in Scotland nationally and internationally. www.braw.org.uk
- Story and National Short Story Prize

SCOTTISH BRAILLE PRESS

Craigmillar Park,
Edinburgh EH16 5NB
Tel: 0131 662 4445
Fax: 0131 662 1968
E-mail: stewart.connell@scottish-braille-press.org
Web site: www.royalblind.org/sbp/or www.scottish-braille-press.org
Contact: Stewart Connell
Description of services: Since its establishment in 1891, the Scottish Braille Press has grown to become one of the world's leading producers of reading material for blind people. As well as printing material for other organisations including the GDBA and NLB, the Scottish Braille Press also publishes The Braille Sporting Record, Madam, Home Help and Spectrum. The Scottish Braille Press also produces braille editions of print bestsellers, tactile diagrams, exam papers, information manuals, audio and large print material.

SCOTTISH DAILY NEWSPAPER SOCIETY, THE

48 Palmerston Place,
Edinburgh EH12 5DE
Tel: 0131 220 4353
Fax: 0131 220 4344
E-mail: info@sdns.org.uk
Contact: J B Raeburn (Director)
Objectives: To promote and represent the interests of publishers of Scottish daily and Sunday newspapers.
Description of services: Lobbying government on issues of direct concern to the industry, self-regulation of the press, Scottish press awards, recognition of advertising agencies and newspaper distribution arrangements.

SCOTTISH POETRY LIBRARY

5 Crichton's Close, Canongate,
Edinburgh EH8 8DT
Tel: 0131 557 2876
Fax: 0131 557 8393
E-mail: inquiries@spl.org.uk
Web site: www.spl.org.uk
Association established: 1982,
Limited company formed 1995
Contacts: Robyn Marsack (Director);
Iain Young (Librarian)
Services offered: Borrowing and
reference library; research assistance
and information; outreach service to
schools, libraries, prisons,
arts/community centres, writers'
groups. Workshops for children in the
library. Thirteen small collections
throughout Scotland.
Description of services: The
Scottish Poetry Library (SPL), a
registered charity open since February
1984, aims to make the poetry of
Scotland, in whatever language, and
a selection of mainly modern poetry
from other countries, visible and freely
accessible to the general public
throughout the country. The resources
and services provided include the
following:

• 20th-century Scottish poetry and
an interesting selection of modern
poetry from all over the world is
available in the library, with older
Scottish poetry also well represented.

• Borrowing is free, apart from a
charge of £1.00 per item borrowed by
post. Freepost return labels are
provided.

• The SPL has a reference
collection of around 15,000 items and
lending stock of around 10,000 items.

• The SPL has pioneered a
computerised index to its poetry
called INSPIRE: International and
Scottish Poetry Information Resource.
This allows people to search for
poetry under their own terms,
controlled by a comprehensive
thesaurus of subjects. Twenty
Scottish literary magazines published
over the past 40 years have also been
indexed and these indexes are
published as The Scottish Poetry
Index. The catalogue is now available
on the web via www.spl.org.uk.

• Current editions of literary
magazines are on sale in the Library
and back numbers may be consulted.

• Audio and video tapes, CDs and
braille items for borrowing and
consulting are also provided. The
stock of these is steadily increasing.

• The SPL Newsletter keeps the
membership in touch. The annual
subscription is £20.00 for individuals
and £30.00 for organisations.

SCOTTISH PRINT EMPLOYERS FEDERATION

48 Palmerston Place,
Edinburgh EH12 5DE
Tel: 0131 220 4353
Fax: 0131 220 4344
E-mail: info@spef.org.uk
Web site: www.spef.org.uk
Contact: J B Raeburn (Director)
Objectives: To promote and represent the interests of the Scottish printing industry.
Description of services: The Federation is the employers' organisation/trade association for all sectors of the printing industry in Scotland. Its principal services embrace industrial relations, education and training, health and safety, productivity and profitability and wages surveys, commercial matters and lobbying on issues of direct concern to the industry.

SCOTTISH PRINTING ARCHIVAL TRUST

3 Zetland Place,
Edinburgh EH5 3HU
Tel: 0131 552 2596
E-mail:
b.clegg@scottishprintarchive.org
Web site:
www.scottishprintarchive.org
Contact: Mr H Bernulf Clegg (Honorary Secretary)
Objectives: To record information, institute research and acquire material relating to the development of Scottish printing for the benefit of the public and print media education.
Description of services: Advisory, informatory and facilitatory.

SCOTTISH ARCHIVE OF PRINT AND PUBLISHING HISTORY RECORDS (SAPPHIRE)

SCOB, Napier University,
Craighouse Campus,
Edinburgh, EH10 5LG.
Tel: 0131 455 6171
Fax: 0131 455 6306
E-mail: scob@napier.ac.uk
Web site: www.sapphire.ac.uk
Contact: Alistair McCleery
Objectives: Sapphire aims to record the social, economic and cultural history of the Scottish printing and publishing industry in the twenty-first century.
Description of services: Sapphire has created a permanent archive of recordings of personal reminiscences of former and current employees within the print and publishing industry. This is complemented by relevant ephemeral material. The archive is available in the Edward Clark Collection at Napier University and also online at www.sapphire.ac.uk

SOCIETY FOR EDITORS AND PROOFREADERS – GLASGOW GROUP

c/o 15 Westbourne Crescent,
Bearsden, Glasgow, G61 4HB
Tel: 0141 942 6338 or 01241 875040
Fax: 0870 133 9436
E-mail: glasgow@sfep.org.uk
Web site: www.sfep-glasgow.org.uk
Contact: Alan Macfarlane or Pat Baxter
Objectives: Members of the SfEP Glasgow Group provide editorial services to our clients across a variety of subjects and formats. We abide by the SfEP Code of Conduct and are committed to excellent standards in editing and in our professional relationship with our clients.
Description of Services: Our members provide freelance editorial services – including copy-editing, on-screen editing, proofreading, indexing, project management, writing, copy-writing, rewriting, music editing/proofreading, research, translating, conference reporting, and web-page design and editing – for a broad spectrum of clients, from mainstream publishing houses to public sector agencies, small businesses, and other non-publishers. We have a wide range of subject interests and specialisms. Clients looking for freelance editorial or proofreading services will almost certainly find someone among us who can provide the expertise they need.

SOCIETY FOR EDITORS AND PROOFREADERS (SFEP)

Riverbank House,
1 Putney Bridge Approach,
Fulham, London SW6 3JD
Tel: 020 7736 3278
Fax: 020 7736 3318
E-mail: administration@sfep.org.uk
Web site: www.sfep.org.uk
Contact: Helen Martin
Objectives: To promote high editorial standards and achieve recognition of the professional status of its members.
Description of services: The SfEP provides its members with a regular newsletter, an annual conference, local meetings and a programme of reasonably priced training courses and professional development days. It produces an annual directory of editorial services containing details of over 500 of its members. The Society supports moves towards recognised standards of training and accreditation for editors and proofreaders, and is currently phasing in its own system of accreditation. The SfEP has close links with the Publishing Training Centre and the Society of Indexers, is represented on the BSI Technical Committee dealing with copy preparation and proof correction (BS 5261), and works to foster good relations with all relevant bodies and organisations in the UK and worldwide.

SOCIETY OF AUTHORS IN SCOTLAND

8 Briar Road, Kirkintilloch,
Glasgow G66 3SA
Tel/fax: 0141 776 4280
E-mail: brian@bdosborne.fsnet.co.uk
Web site: www.societyofauthors.com
Contact: Brian D Osborne
(Honorary Secretary)
Objectives: Founded to represent, assist and protect writers.
Description of services: The Society (Headquarters: 84 Drayton Gardens, London SW10 9SB.
Tel: 020 7373 6642. **Fax:** 020 7373 5768) is an independent trade union, representing writers' interests in all aspects of the writing profession, including book and periodical publishing, new media, broadcasting, television and films and has now almost 500 members in Scotland. The Society of Authors has specialist groups for broadcasters, children's writers, translators, medical, scientific and technical writers and illustrators. The Society of Authors in Scotland organises talks and lectures, social events and visits to places offering research opportunities for members, bookshop events open to the public and each year provides a very popular strand of practical talks and workshops 'The Writing Business' at the Edinburgh International Book Festival.

SOCIETY OF INDEXERS (SCOTTISH GROUP)

c/o Ballechin Home Farm,
Ballinluig, Pitlochry,
Perthshire PH9 0LW
Tel/Fax: 01887 840 259/ 01887 840735
E-mail: paulnash@zetnet.co.uk
Contact: Paul Nash
Objectives: The Scottish Group represents the Society locally. It aims to promote indexing amongst Scottish publishers and authors and to provide a forum for indexers.

Description of services: Contact point for everyone interested in the indexing of books, periodicals and other materials. Meetings and training sessions for members. Our local directory – Indexers Available in Scotland – is published and circulated biennially; it lists indexers and their specialised subjects.

ISBN, SAN AND DOI AGENCY

3rd Floor, Midas House,
62 Goldsworth Road,
Woking GU21 6LQ
Tel: 0870 777 8712
Fax: 0870 777 8714
E-mail: isbn@nielsenbookdata.co.uk, san@nielsenbookdata.co.uk, doi@nielsenbookdata.co.uk
Web site:
www.isbn.nielsenbookdata.co.uk
www.sanagency.co.uk
www.doi.nielsenbookdata.co.uk
Objectives: Nielsen BookData Registration Services provide UK and other English-language publishers with a range of standard identifiers for use in the international supply chain.

Description of services: The ISBN Agency issues ISBNs to publishers based in the UK and the Republic of Ireland.

The SAN Agency is administered on behalf of the Book Industry Communication. It assigns Standard Address Numbers and Global Location Numbers for organisations in any country except USA, Canada, Australia and New Zealand.

The DOI Agency provides web-based registration and maintenance facilities for DOIs and their metadata for use by any publisher regardless of their location.

WIGTOWN BOOK TOWN COMPANY

Wigtown Book Town Company
County Buildings,
Wigtown DG8 9JH
Tel: 01988 402 036
Fax: 01988 402 506
E-mail:
john@wigtown-booktown.co.uk
Contact: John Robertson (Project Manager)
Web site:
www.wigtown-booktown.co.uk
Date of Book Festival: The Wigtown Booktown is a bi-annual event in May and September.
22nd September – 1st October 2006
The Scottish Book Town Festival is a 10-day celebration of the written word in Wigtown, our National Book Town. Normally home to only 900 people, a malt whisky distillery and a quarter of a million books, the Wigtown Festival prompts a mass migration of bibliophiles to this green, pastoral corner of Scotland.

All our venues are warm and dry, and offer the ideal refuge from an autumnal shower. And rest assured that, between events, there will be plenty of time to soak up the atmosphere in Scotland's widest street or browse around our cavernous bookshops.

Please keep an eye on the web site for advance details as the programme develops. If you are not already on our database and would like to receive a free copy of the programme – please e-mail us at mail@wigtownbookfestival.com with your details.

Services

Working freelance *Kate Blackadder*

Many of the small publishing companies in Scotland cannot afford to employ full-time staff. Some larger companies are also reluctant to employ a full complement of in-house staff as they face pressure to reduce fixed costs.

This means that many more publishing professionals now work on a freelance basis, either from choice or necessity. There are more opportunities, but there is also more competition for the work. Many who build a successful career in this way are highly motivated, highly trained and experienced, and have spent time building good contacts. Many people find it an ideal working lifestyle, but it is important to have the relevant skills and ability to deliver what the publisher needs, to a standard, on time and at a price agreeable to both sides.

Skills and training

Many freelancers are expected to have at least some formal training in their field, either from courses or in-house. Some will have been made redundant from full-time jobs. Many of the establishments in the Publishing Training section on pp.70-71 run short courses, and organisations like the Society for Editors and Proofreaders run training courses for freelancers – including one called Going Freelance (see p.120).

Pros and Cons

Anyone considering working freelance should weigh up the following before committing to self-employment. Advantages might include: being your own boss; working hours which suit you – this may include fitting in with looking after children; increased financial rewards (a person working full time on an equivalent salary to a self-employed person will earn less because of fewer tax breaks); no office politics; no commuting; a sense of independence and freedom. Disadvantages might include: a feeling of isolation through working alone; lack of self-discipline; no fixed holiday allowance; no holiday pay or sick pay; working weekends and public holidays; reluctance to turn down jobs, especially at the beginning; a lack of separation between work and home life, especially if you are based in your living room; no corporate benefits such as a pension; fluctuating income and, finally, a lot of time spent doing the books and chasing payment of invoices.

Although there seem to be more possible disadvantages than benefits, if successful, freelance work can be extremely rewarding and stimulating, particularly as your client base extends and you find yourself working for a variety of different companies. With a core of regular clients, your income will become more stable.

Freelancers working from home may go through long periods of having very little contact with other people. There are a number of organisations that provide a forum for freelancers to meet, for example, the Society of Editors and Proofreaders, which has local groups and annual conferences.

Starting Off

It may be difficult to get started as a freelancer as employers tend to use people they already know. It is imperative, therefore, that any work carried out is accurate and done on time, as this will encourage publishers to give you further work and perhaps recommend you to others. Ensure that you have a contact at the company with whom you can discuss any problems and to whom you can apply for further work. Freelancers are generally supportive of each other so any chance you get to talk with others can often lead to a commission or fresh ideas on how to acquire new clients.

Fees

Depending upon the publisher, fees for specific jobs can vary. Both the National Union of Journalists and the Society of Editors and Proofreaders recommend minimum hourly rates for editorial work, but you should be prepared to be flexible. For example, the biggest companies don't necessarily pay the biggest fees but you might want their name on your CV. Don't undervalue yourself, though, or others will too. Many publishers are keen to work on a 'fixed fee' basis,

whereby the fee is negotiated between publisher and freelancer. You should calculate a minimum hourly rate for yourself, carefully, ensuring that it covers all your costs, and that it is realistic and competitive. If you start the job and find that for some reason it is going to take longer than estimated, alert the publisher immediately to discuss the problem.

Practical matters

When you become self-employed, you must inform your local tax office, and the Contributions Agency. You are responsible for paying your own tax and you should set aside a third of your income to meet the Inland Revenue's deadlines for each tax year. Fines for late payments are high and interest is charged.

It is also advisable to negotiate an overdraft facility with your bank at the outset to allow for expenditure that is incurred before you have been paid by clients. You may have to invest in, or update, a computer. Ideally this should be the best you can afford, with current, industry-standard software, and e-mail connection. Sometimes the Inland Revenue offers tax breaks on the purchase of computer hardware to those who are registered as self-employed.

If you are intending to use part of your house as an office you may have to adapt a room for the purpose (and don't forget to inform your house contents insurer). Good lighting is important, particularly if you are carrying out any work that involves checking colour. Setting aside a specific area in the house can help you concentrate and prevent a collision between work and home-life.

You can offset all business expenses against your income thereby reducing your tax liability, so keep all receipts and check with your accountant or the Inland Revenue on what exactly you can claim for. On the subject of accountants – you can, of course, complete your own Self-Assessment Tax Form but an accountant, or tax consultant, will keep you right and have up-to-date information. Some accountants work from home themselves so will be less expensive than a large firm and can actually save you money. If this is an area that is new to you, an accountant can help you establish a system of simple book-keeping. The more accurate your own records are, the less it will cost you in accountancy fees. Ask established freelancers for recommendations.

Be aware that securing a mortgage may not be easy once you become self-employed, even with trading accounts behind you – three years' accounts are usually asked for – but some banks are more sympathetic than others so it is worth shopping around. Financial provision for retirement is a priority, given the state provision that currently exists. This may or may not take the form of a personal pension. Some form of health insurance is essential too. Your accountant should be able to point you in the direction of an independent financial advisor who can advise you.

Services

Copy-editing and proofreading *Kate Blackadder*

Copy-editing

Copy-editing is the process by which prelim pages, text, illustrations, tables and any other matter are checked in preparation for publication. Its main aims are to eliminate any potential obstacles between the reader and what the author wants to convey, and to save time and money by solving problems before the book goes any further. The copy-editing process involves a number of editing forms and can involve a range of personnel both in-house and externally in the form of freelancers. Editing can be done on hard copy or, increasingly, on-screen. The main forms of editing are: substantive editing, editing for sense and consistency, and editing in preparation for typesetting.

Substantive editing

This involves the editor organising, and aiming to improve, the presentation of the content, scope, length and level of a piece of writing. This may involve asking the author to rewrite, reconstruct, look for more or different pictures etc. At this stage the editor will also look out for potentially libellous or defamatory material.

Editing for sense and consistency

Here the text is examined in detail to ensure that the meaning is clear and as the author intended. The editor checks that grammar, spelling (check with the publisher to see if they favour one dictionary over another) and punctuation are correct and consistent; that captions are correct, chapter titles are consistent with the contents page, and that tables, notes and cross-references are referred to accurately. This may be either according to the editor's own style or the publisher's house style (see also House style, below). At this stage, the editor will also look out for quotations or illustrations that require copyright clearance and, if so, seek formal permission from the relevant source.

Editing for presentation to typesetter

This involves making sure the material is complete and clearly identifiable: quoted matter highlighted as being separate from the main text; heading levels checked; illustrations and tables placed. To work effectively and economically the typesetter has to be able to read the typescript clearly. Any obstacles such as post-it labels or quirky signs will cause delays and add to costs. The standard signs used for marking up the typescript can be found in British Standard 5261 Marks for Copy Preparation and Proof Correction which can be obtained from the British Standards Institute.

Proofreading

There are three ways of checking proofs. The first is reading for sense (sometimes referred to as 'blind' proofreading) which does not involve looking at the original typescript but means checking the proofs by themselves for errors in spelling, punctuation and so on, noting in pencil or on a separate sheet any queries for the copy-editor or author to answer. (It may be useful here to remember this: **Q.** How many proofreaders does it take to change a light bulb? **A.** Proofreaders aren't supposed to change light bulbs – only query them.) The second way is to read for sense while also checking details such as dates against the typescript. The third way is to check everything against the typescript with a separate read of the proof on its own since it is difficult to check for sense and for details at the same time. This third way is essential when the book has been presented to the publisher in a traditional way, that is, not on disk but in a manuscript that has subsequently been sent out to a typesetter.

In the traditional way also a colour code is used by proofreaders to distinguish between publisher's and author's errors and errors made by the typesetter: typesetter's error – red ink, author's or publisher's – blue or black ink. (Even more traditionally, when typesetters read proofs before sending them out they would mark their own mistakes in green.) The reason for this distinction is that the typesetter will pay for their errors while the publisher will be charged for their own or their author's errors. In modern practice, however, these distinctions are blurred – for example, it may be the designer who takes in

the corrections without distinguishing fault – so it is important to get a good brief from the publisher so that you are clear about what you are required to do.

First proofs

First proofs used to be in the form of a continuous sheet and were called galley proofs; they have been generally replaced by first page proofs. The proofreader's job is to check the proofs in one of the ways described in the previous two paragraphs. Usually the author reads a set of page proofs at the same time, and the in-house editor will check and collate corrections from both sides, but it might be that the freelance editor controls this side of things also. If the book is to have an index, it is compiled at this stage. Prelims should be prepared now, if this has not already happened, and they, with the master set of proofs, should be sent back to the typesetter.

Further proofs

At second proof stage the proofreader will check the first proof of the index and check that corrections from the first proofs have been made. Page set-up, pagination and headings should be read and checked for position, spelling and accuracy. Depending on the level of corrections, the second set of page proofs might be the last and final set before the job goes onto a disk for the printer.

House style
A house style is a set of rules adopted by a publishing company which covers spelling, punctuation, abbreviations, numerals, capitalisation, parochialisms etc. The editorial department will establish a house style and any freelancers and authors will be provided with a style sheet to follow. The objective is to maintain a consistent typographical and grammatical style throughout the text. If the publisher does not provide a style sheet the best thing to do is to follow the author's own conventions provided they are clear and make common sense.

Prelim pages
Prelim pages are the parts of the book that precede the main body of the text. Prelim pages include: the title page, which provides details of the series title if necessary, the title of the book, the subtitle, the author or editor and the translator and the illustrator if applicable; the other side of the title page (the 'title verso') which must include the name and address of the publisher, the name of the printer, the edition if other than the first, the date of publication, the ISBN (International Standard Book Number, see also Copyright section p. 00 and Organisations section p. 00) and a line on CIP (British Library Cataloguing in Publication) data; and, if necessary, a half-title page (containing the title only), acknowledgements, picture credits, dedication and

chapter/illustration contents pages.

In-house the copy-editor may be responsible for obtaining an ISBN, CIP data and asserting the moral rights of the author.

Indexing
The function of an index is to assist the reader to gain quick access to selected material within the book. It is, therefore, extremely important for the index to be accurate and easy to use. The compilation of an index may be undertaken by the author, the editor or a professional indexer. (See Society of Indexers, p.122) The editor has to decide which person is best equipped to index the title in question. For example, the author may understand the subject and the needs of the reader better than a professional but lack technical indexing skills.

Further reading
Butcher, Judith, *Copy-editing: The Cambridge Handbook for Editors, Authors and Publishers*, 3rd ed, Cambridge University Press, 1992
Harris, Nicola, *Basic Editing: A Practical Course*, 2 vols, *The Text and The Exercises*, Book House Training Centre, 1991
Hart's Rules for Compositors and Readers at the University Press, Oxford, 39th ed, 1993
The Chambers Dictionary, Chambers, *9th ed, 2003*
Jarvie, Gordon, *Grammar Guide*, Bloomsbury, 1999
Bryson, Bill, *The Penguin Dictionary of Troublesome Words*, Penguin, 1988
Walsh, Bill, *Lapsing into a Comma: a curmudgeon's guide to the many things than can go wrong in print – and how to avoid them*, Contemporary Books, 2000
Crystal, David, *Language and the Internet*, Cambridge University Press, 2001
Truss, Lynne, *Eats, Shoots and Leaves: The Zero Tolerance Approach to Punctuation*, Profile Books, 2003

Services

Design

MARK BLACKADDER
39 Warrender Park Terrace,
Edinburgh EH9 1EB
Tel: 0131 228 4237
E-mail:
m.blackadder@btopenworld.com
Qualifications and experience:
Diploma in Art and Design. 26 years'
graphic design experience, 15 of
which as freelance.
Equipment: Apple Mac.
Clients include: ASLS, Birlinn Ltd,
Malcolm Cant Publications, Dunedin
Academic Press, EUP, Fort
Publishing, W. Green, Mercat Press,
NMS Enterprises – Publishing, Neil
Wilson Publishing, Scottish Publishers
Association.
Services offered: The internal and
external design of books.

CALEB RUTHERFORD – eidetic
5 West Stanhope Place,
Edinburgh EH12 5HQ
Tel: 0131 337 9724
Fax: 0131 623 1244
E-mail:
caleb.eidetic@blueyonder.co.uk
eidetic, a business with an
outstanding track record, provides
creative design and project
management. Working principally in
design for print across publishing,
retail and corporate industries. Our
aim is to provide our clients with the
highest quality design and to manage
projects efficiently to meet schedules
and budgets.

HAMPTON-SMITH LTD

PO Box 6721
Fochabers
Moray
IV32 7YH
Tel: 01343 870 012
E-mail: sales@hampton-smith.com
Web site: www.hampton-smith.com
Qualifications and experience:
Five years working in the publishing
industry on design and typesetting.
Services offered:
- Typesetting
- Cover design
- All printed material design eg
  brochures, leaflets, letterheads
- Web site design
- E-commerce

IAN KIRKWOOD DESIGN

Coire Menach, Kirkmichael,
Blairgowrie, Perthshire,
PH10 7NB
Tel: 01250 881 434
Fax: 01250 881 434
E-mail: ian@ik-design.co.uk
Web site: www.ik-design.co.uk
Qualifications and experience: Ian
Kirkwood has a BA Hons degree in
Design from Edinburgh College of Art.
He was a designer with the National
Trust for Scotland, working on guide
books and magazines etc.
International magazine work and
cover/typographic designs for recent
Scottish titles. Enquiries welcome.
Equipment and services offered:
Mac based publishing.
Book/magazine design, as well as
illustration (He has illustrated children's
books in print).

Services

Editorial

AMBERTEXT
(Sandy Nicholson)
2/GF Bruntsfield Crescent,
Edinburgh,
EH10 4EZ
Tel: 0131 447 9257
E-mail: sandy@ambertext.co.uk
Web site: www.ambertext.co.uk
Qualifications and experience:
MA Physics, BSc Hons Mathematics
(class 1); five years' postgraduate
mathematics research (functional
analysis); six years' technical writing
experience; training in editing and
proofreading by the Society for
Editors and Proofreaders (courses in
editing mathematics and music) and
The Publishing Training Centre
(distinction in Basic Proofreading).
Recent work: proofreading a series
of A-level mathematics textbooks for
Pearson Education; editing and
proofreading various books and
transcripts for the Open University;
editing and typesetting organ pieces
for Kevin Mayhew Publishers.
Services offered: Copy-editing and
proofreading, with particular expertise
in mathematics and music. On-screen
editing/typesetting in TeX (for
mathematical material), Sibelius (for
music), Adobe InDesign and Microsoft
Word. Subjects: mathematics,
computer science, physics, music,
philosophy, logic, linguistics, Gaelic
(typesetting and basic proofreading
only); any other subject area
considered. Books, journals, sheet
music, software manuals, web sites,
newsletters etc.

KATE BLACKADDER
39 Warrender Park Terrace,
Edinburgh EH9 1EB
Tel/fax: 0131 228 4237
Qualifications and experience:
Diploma in Book and Periodical
Publishing. Over 20 years' publishing
experience in-house and freelance in
London and Edinburgh. Member of
the Society of Editors and
Proofreaders.
Services offered: Copy-editing and
proofreading general non-fiction,
fiction, children's books and corporate
literature. Abridging books and short
stories.
Clients include: Birlinn Ltd, Random
House, Scottish Arts Council, Scottish
Consumer Council, Neil Wilson
Publishing, Radio Scotland, Radio 4,
Scottish Natural Heritage, Scottish
Publishers Association and Whittles
Publishing.

BOOKPRINT CREATIVE SERVICES

2a The Avenue
Eastbourne
East Sussex
BN21 3YA
Tel: 01323 411 315
E-mail: BCS@bookprint.co.uk
Web site: www.bookprint.co.uk
Company established: 1993
Contacts: David Nickalls
and Tim Short
Services offered: Since 1993 we
have designed and produced many
hundreds of titles for publishers, from
mass-market paperbacks to complex
bibles (i.e most types of book except
full-colour). We offer a complete one-
stop service from receipt of text to
delivery of finished books, and in
addition can provide editorial services,
sales, marketing and distribution. We
offer flexibility, fast schedules and
reduced rates for regular/volume
work. We are an independent
company founded on 30 years'
experience, and provide a high quality
professional service for publishers
large and small. Please visit our web
site to see how we can assist you.

ALISON BOWERS

49 Mayfield Road,
Edinburgh EH9 2NQ
Tel: 0131 667 8317
E-mail: AliBowers@blueyonder.co.uk
Qualifications and experience:
Hons English degree. Five years on
Pergamon/Elsevier linguistics encyclo-
pedia: commissioning, author–editor
liaison, editing, writing, translation
(French). Textbook project-editing and
copy-editing, all subject areas, from
original MS via all stages to collation.
Clients include: Churchill
Livingstone/Harcourt, Routledge,
Pearson, OUP, Universities of
Edinburgh and London. PhD and LLM
students, intending authors.
Services offered: Project editing:
author liaison, copy-editing all stages;
thesis editing, student consultation.
Proofreading English, French,
Spanish. Subject areas: all
literary/humanities, linguistics, social
science, medicine, law.

MARY BRAILEY

Ballagan Cottage,
Strathblane,
Glasgow G63 9AE
Tel: 01360 771 613
E-mail: info@the-word-shop.co.uk
Web site: www.the-word-shop.co.uk
Qualifications and experience:
Four years' experience as freelance
proofreader and editor, working for
publishers, government agencies,
voluntary organisations, businesses
and individual writers. BA Latin (First),
Diploma in Housing, Certificate in
Social Work Management, PTC
proofreading course (distinction),
trained in copy-editing, web editing,
web design, on-screen editing,
creative writing. Advanced member of
the Society for Editors and
Proofreaders. Previously worked in
housing and social work, in local
authorities, voluntary organisations
and universities.
Equipment and software: PC,
scanner/copier, word processing,
spreadsheets, web page authoring,
graphics.
Services offered: Research,
proofreading, editing, writing, re-
writing, summarising. Aim to help
clients to achieve excellence in their
written publications for print or the
web. Will take on most subjects, but
specialist knowledge of housing,
social work, social policy, equalities,
management and related subjects.

GILLIAN CLOKE

16 Buckstone Close,
Edinburgh EH10 6NW
Tel: 0131 662 0644
E-mail: gill.cloke@virgin.net
Qualifications and experience:
MA (Hons) MPhil (Humanities). 10
years publishing experience in-house
(Scottish Christian Press and Elsevier
Health Professions) and freelance, in
all areas of commissioning, editing
and project development.
Equipment: Windows XP supporting
Microsoft Word, Office and Excel – I
don't have DTP packages – but do
have Broadband.
Services offered: Complete range
of publishing services –
troubleshooting a specialty! Editing,
writing/rewriting, research, proof
correction, indexing, reference
checking; on-screen or hard copy.
Particularly at home in the history,
classical, literature & humanities,
religious, and education, experienced
also in medical and musical;
competent in classical languages, and
in medical, legal and ecclesiastical
Latin.

CHARLES S COVENTRY

23/9 Viewcraig Street,
Edinburgh EH8 9UJ
Tel: 0131 558 8785
E-mail: charlie_cov@yahoo.co.uk
Web site:
www.geocities.com/charlie_cov
Qualifications and experience:
MA, BPhil, MLitt, Dip TEFL.
Proofreader including work on Gaelic
texts for Polygon; part of textbook on
spiritual development for Floris Books;
Teach Yourself Ancient Greek for
Hodder & Stoughton Educational;
SVC Gaelic Learners Higher Still
course book; indexer, not fully trained;
community newspapers; voluntary
proofreading for Dumbiedykes
newsletter News 'n' Views. Volunteer
office support, proofreading and word
processing services for Gay Men's
Health, 10b Union Street, Edinburgh.
Most proofreading is for magazine
Core. Also check consistency of
language (medical or colloquial) for
information on web site. One
commission for Scottish Executive.
Gaelic translation of letter from First
Minister for cultural exchange to USA.
Equipment: Computer IBM
compatible, MS Word, MS Publisher,
scanner and photocopier on site.

Services offered: Proofreading,
general coverage; indexing arts
subjects, particularly linguistics; also
local and community newspapers.
Compiled abstract of own thesis,
edited piece about green spaces for
newsletter. Proofreading; indexing;
translation, English to Gaelic, Gaelic
to English; French to English or
Gaelic; Latin to English. Also, for
overseas students, proofreading and
checking English in theses; 1996
thesis for Korean Law student
checked. In 2005, proofreading for
Mainstream, 'A Waxing Moon', story
of Sabhal Mor Ostaig.

HISTORY IN THE MAKING

(Heritage Consultants)
220 Deeside Gardens,
Aberdeen AB15 7PS
Tel: 01224 200 302
Fax: 01224 315 194
E-mail: grant@historymakers.co.uk
Web site: www.historymakers.co.uk
Qualifications and experience:
Partners: Grant G Simpson MA
(Hons), PhD, FSA: formerly Reader in
Scottish History, Aberdeen University;
author/editor of numerous
books/articles on Scottish history and
records; experienced in archaeology,
print design and archive adminis-
tration. Ms Anne T Simpson MA
(Hons), MCIM, qualified in marketing,
business administration; experience in
museum curatorship; teaching,
lecturing, writing.
Equipment: iMac, HP Laser Printer,
Filemaker 5.5
Services offered: Centred on
Scottish history, in widest terms, with
provision of fully researched, accurate
and clearly presented material over all
periods and topics. Historical research
and copywriting, visitor display
presentation, translation (Latin and
Scots), transcriptions of early
documents, media consultancy (film,
video, television), archive cataloguing,
proofreading, and indexing for those
clients who see the advantage of
manually produced indexes.

BILL HOUSTON

4 Cranston Drive,
Cousland,
Dalkeith EH22 2PP
Tel: 0131 663 1238
E-mail:
williamhouston@amserve.com
Qualifications and experience:
BSc (Hons), DipLib, MPhil, Chartered
Biologist, 30 years' experience.
Services offered: Comprehensive
editorial service, from manuscript
preparation through to final proofs,
including collation. All-year-round
service. Specialist in medical and
scientific texts. Originally sub-editor
with Elsevier in Amsterdam; 30
years'experience as a full-time
freelance editor. Sub-editing,
proofreading, re-writing, abstracting,
book reviewing. Numerous clients
throughout the UK.

DUNCAN MCARA

(*see also literary agents*)
28 Beresford Gardens
Edinburgh EH5 3ES
Tel/fax: 0131 552 1558
E-mail: duncanmcara@hotmail.com
Qualifications and experience:
Diploma in Publishing. Over 30 years'
publishing experience in-house (John
Murray and Faber & Faber) in London
and freelance in Edinburgh.
Equipment: Windows XP; Microsoft
Office Word 2000.
Services offered: Editorial
consultant on all aspects of trade
publishing. Editing, re-writing, copy-
editing, proof correction for
publishers, financial companies,
academic institutions and other
organisations.

MANDY MACDONALD

54 Duthie Terrace,
Aberdeen AB10 7PR
Tel/fax: 01224 326 143
E-mail: MacMand44@aol.com
Qualifications and experience:
MA (Cantab.), Classics; Dip.Mus.
(CCAT); LRCM. Freelance 1975-9 and
1987 to present. Member, SfEP
(Glasgow Group)
Clients include: Aberdeen
University, International
Correspondents in Education, Women
in Development Europe, UK Gender
and Development Network, Whitaker's
Scottish Almanack, United Nations
University Press, ILO, International
Atomic Energy Agency, British and
European development aid agencies.
Cambridge University Press and other
UK publishers.
Services offered: Writing/research
(inc. articles, reports, briefings, guides,
background research for media
projects); rewriting (inc. adaptation of
specialised research for a general
audience); copy-editing/proofreading
on hard copy and screen, including
foreign languages (Spanish, French,
Italian, Latin) and music; translating
(Spanish, French into English);
management of editorial projects (inc.
newsletters, multi-author books),
conference reporting. Main subject
areas: humanities, social sciences
(especially Latin America),
international development,
gender/women's studies, human

rights, music. Authoritative, accurate, literate, readable texts produced. Deadlines met. Consultation with clients a priority. Will travel for short in-house contracts.

MAKAR PUBLISHING PRODUCTION

David McLeod,
12 Corstorphine High Street,
Edinburgh, EH12 7ST
Tel: 0131 334 3693
Mob: 0770 841 5911
E-mail: dzmcleod@yahoo.co.uk
Experience: 30 years of extensive publishing production and design experience. Clients along the way have included: Mainstream Publishing, Dunedin Academic Press, Heinemann, Churches Together in Britain and Ireland, John Murray, Penguin, University Press of the West Indies, Overseas Development Agency (ODA), The Partnership. Project management from copy-writing to print-buying, producing and designing and commissioning for kids book, cook books, large format colour-integrated co-editions, catalogues, corporate reports, postage-stamp issues, all sorts of books and beyond.
Services Offered:
Using industry standard publishing software (Quark, InDesign, Photoshop, etc.), Makar provides publishing project management from concept to finished book, complete publication design and typesetting. Hand-knitted publishing solutions to fit your schedule and budget.

SUSAN MILLIGAN

39 Cecil Street (3/l),
Glasgow G12 8RN
Tel: 0141 334 2807
E-mail: susan@writtenword.co.uk
Qualifications and experience:
MA (Hons), PhD. Training in editing
and proofreading by SPA, Society for
Editors and Proofreaders (SfEP) and
the Publishing Training Centre (Basic
Editing, pass with distinction).
Advanced member of SfEP.
Equipment: PC, MS Word, colour
inkjet printer, scanner.
Services offered: Copy-editing and
proofreading general non-fiction,
academic and reference works,
including multi-author volumes
involving project management.
Handling of illustrated British history
and local history books, from copy-
editing through to final proofs. Editing,
at all levels, of reports and company
publications. Experience in research
and writing (published author). Wide
range of subject interests, including
education, religion and humanities,
especially history, classics, ancient
languages and civilisations.

JENNIE RENTON EDITORIAL

Main Point Books,
8 Lauriston Street,
Edinburgh EH3 9DJ
Tel: 0131 228 4837
E-mail: the.editor@textualities.net
Services offered: All aspects of
book production undertaken – editing,
proofreading, copywriting, typesetting,
etc.

MAIRI SUTHERLAND

36 Claremont Road,
Edinburgh EH6 7NH
Tel: 0131 555 1848
Fax: 0131 555 6943
E-mail: mairi.s@ednet.co.uk

Qualifications and experience:
MA (Hons) Mathematics and
Philosophy; Cert. Ed.; over 20 years'
editorial experience in-house and
freelance; also lecturer in editing;
examiner for the Society for Editors
and Proofreaders (SfEP); SfEP
Advanced Member and accredited
proofreader.

Clients include: Birlinn, Cambridge
University Press, Canongate, Hodder
& Stoughton, Macmillan, Learning and
Teaching Scotland, Scottish Wildlife
Trust, Scottish Executive.

Equipment: Apple Macintosh
(Word, PageMaker, Adobe Acrobat).

Services offered: Project
management; editing; on-screen
editing; re-writing; proofreading (hard
copy and on-screen); consultancy;
training. Subject areas include: arts
and social science, astronomy,
biography, children's, conservation,
education, fiction, geography,
mathematics, natural history,
philosophy, science, travel, wildlife.
Media: books (including highly
illustrated), company literature
(brochures, reports), journals,
manuals, newsletters, magazines.

SCOTT RUSSELL PUBLISHING SERVICES

12 Arundel Drive
Battlefield
Glasgow G42 9RF
Tel: 07834 237 133
E-mail: info@scottrussell.co.uk
Web site: www.scottrussell.co.uk

Qualifications and experience:
MA English Literature, Diploma
Information and library studies, MLitt
Publishing studies.

Over 15 years' experience in both
the repro and newspaper sectors. As
an IT manager I devised, implemented
and supported complex digital
workflows in The Herald, Evening
Times and Sunday Herald
newspapers. With Guardian
Newspapers Ltd I carried out system
testing and delivered end-user
training. I have presented to IFRA on
digital asset management and I also
hold the CIPD Certificate in Training
Practice.

Services offered:
Productivity, management and
technical services tailored to large and
small-scale publishers, including:

- Advice on managing your
  electronic workflow by improving
  file management, versioning and
  collaboration
- Evaluation of your business
  requirements
- Project management for
  upgrading or moving to new
  systems.

- Advice on software tools, picture management, image adjustment and archiving.
- Training in desktop publishing applications including Adobe InDesign, Photoshop and QuarkXPress as well as Macintosh OS X.
- Technical assistance with installation and maintenance of systems.

TEVIOTDALE PUBLISHING SOLUTIONS
18 Teviotdale Place
Edinburgh
EH3 5HY
Tel: 0131 332 3418
E-mail: TPS@teviotdale.demon.co.uk
Qualifications and Experience:
Teviotdale Publishing Solutions is an editorial and publishing consultancy run by two experienced academic and educational publishers, Fiona McDonald and Tony Wayte. We have more than 30 years experience as editors and publishers in the UK and Australia, having worked for market-leading publishers such as OUP, Chapman and Hall, Blackwell and Harcourt Education/Reed Education. This professional expertise is supported by strong academic backgrounds in the humanities and sciences.

Services offered: As an editorial and publishing consultancy, we can offer a full range of services to help publishers, including:
- full project management (from initial concept to printer-ready files)
- list development
- commissioning of projects
- author briefing
- manuscript development
- managing and coordinating multi-component and highly illustrated series

- freelance design contacts
- editing and proof-reading
- market research and competition analysis

If you have too much to do, and not enough time or people to do it all, we can help!

Services

Illustration

SCOTTISH ILLUSTRATORS

11a Gayfield Studios
Gayfield Square
Edinburgh
EH1 3NT
E-mail: info@scottishillustrators.com
web site:
www.scottishillustrators.com
contact: Alan McGowan
scottishillustrators.com is a web site
created to make accessing Scottish
illustrators easier. It has been
developed to create one central
space where freelance illustrators are
gathered together so that art directors
can see what is available, and also to
provide a forum and focal point for
Scottish illustration.

The site contains examples of
work, links to illustrators home pages
and direct contact information for
each illustrator: it is NOT an agency,
takes no percentage on jobs commissioned, and does not charge
designers a fee to use the site.

This web site exists to make more
visible the diverse and unique wealth
of illustration talent in Scotland. The
site promotes about 50 highly professional illustrators throughout Scotland,
who work in a variety of mediums
such as watercolour, pen and ink,
collage, painting and styles such as
children's, natural history, technical,
cartoons, and more.

Services

Indexing

JANE ANGUS
Darroch Den,
Hawthorn Place,
Ballater AB35 5QH
Tel: 0133 97 56260
E-mail: jane.angus@homecall.co.uk
Qualifications and experience:
Geologist with indexing experience in
geology (both petroleum and environ-
mental), natural history, environmental
studies, ecology, agriculture, forestry,
aquaculture, Scottish archaeology,
general Scottish affairs.
Equipment: IBM compatible PC
Macrex 7 Indexing programme;
abstracting.
  Receive and send hard copy and
or disc, or electronically.

INDX LTD (ANNE SOLAMITO)
3 Coast, Inverasdale,
Poolewe,
Ross-shire IV22 2LR
Tel: 01445 781438
E-mail: solamito@btinternet.com
Qualifications and experience:
BA (Hons), PG Dip Lib, Society of
Indexers accreditation.
Equipment: Macrex (indexing
software), Microsoft Word, Excel.
Services offered: Indexing; book
research; abstracting; translation;
classifying; word processing and
proofreading.

ANNE MCCARTHY
Bentfield,
3 Marine Terrace,
Gullane,
East Lothian EH31 2AY
Tel/fax: 01620 842 247
E-mail:
annemccarthy@btinternet.com
Qualifications and experience:
MA, registered indexer, over 30 years'
experience.
Equipment: PC and specialised
indexing program.
Services offered: Small or large
indexes undertaken. Particular
interests: medical sciences, Scottish
history, culture and language, local
history, sport, travel and guide-books,
biography and reference works.

Services

Literary Agents

JENNY BROWN ASSOCIATES
33 Argyle Place
Edinburgh EH9 1JT
Tel: 0131 229 5334
E-mail:
jenny-brown@blueyonder.co.uk or
mstan@blueyonder.co.uk
Web site:
www.jennybrownassociates.com
Services offered: Literary agency
(established 2002) representing 50
writers of literary fiction, non-fiction,
and crime writing. Most of the
agency's clients are based in Scotland
which allows a close working
relationship between writer and agent,
but the company sells work to
publishers worldwide. Please see web
site for submission details.

FRASER ROSS ASSOCIATES
6 Wellington Place,
Edinburgh EH6 7EQ
Contacts: Lindsey Fraser,
Kathryn Ross
Tel: 0131 553 2759
and 0131 657 4412
Fax: 0131 553 2759
E-mail: lindsey.fraser@tiscali.co.uk
and kjross@tiscali.co.uk
Services offered: Literary Agency,
Literary Consultancy; Literary Project
Management; Outreach and training
in readership development, with an
emphasis on reading with young
people.

DUNCAN MCARA
(*also see Editorial*)
28 Beresford Gardens
Edinburgh EH5 3ES
Tel/fax: 0131 552 1558
E-mail: duncanmcara@hotmail.com
Qualifications and experience:
Diploma in Publishing. Over 30 years'
publishing experience in-house (John
Murray and Faber & Faber) in London
and freelance in Edinburgh.
Equipment: Windows XP; Microsoft
Office Word 2000.
Services offered: Literary agent for
literary fiction; non-fiction: art,
architecture, archaeology, biography,
military, travel, Scottish interest.
Preliminary letter with SAE essential.
No reading fee.
Commission: Home 10%; US 15%;
translation 20%

Services

Marketing and Public Relations

COLMAN GETTY SCOTLAND PR
5 Gayfield Square,
Edinburgh EH1 3NW
Contacts: Rebecca Salt,
Nicky Stonehill and Fiona Atherton
Tel: 0131 558 8851
Fax: 0131 558 8852
E-mail: nicky@colmangettypr.co.uk
Web site: www.colmangettypr.co.uk
Qualifications and experience:
PR specialists in publishing and the arts.
Services offered: UK-wide media relations, copywriting, launch events, event management, profile management. Offices in London and Edinburgh.

IE PARTNERS LTD
The Barley Mow Centre
10 Barley Mow Passage
London W4 4PH
Tel: + 44 (0)20 8996 1766
E-mail: enquiries@iepartners.co.uk
Web site: www.iepartners.co.uk
Contacts: Tony Read, Tania Bapuji, Amanda Buchan, David Foster, Andy Smart, Vincent Bontoux (Paris office)
IE Partners (International Education Partners) provides consultancy, advisory, research and training services to international agencies, governments, trade bodies and commercial organisations throughout the world. The work is focused in particular on book provision issues including the supply of books and other teaching and learning materials through aid-funded programmes in developing countries. The staff of IE Partners travel extensively, working on aid-funded projects and maintain good contacts in the book trade in many countries.

IE Partners can advise on international publishing and book trade issues and may be retained to undertake research on appropriate opportunities in any country.

JAN RUTHERFORD
Publicity and the Printed Word
5 West Stanhope Place,
Edinburgh EH12 5HQ
Tel: 0131 337 9724/07710 474 308
Fax: 0131 623 1244
E-mail: jan.ppw@blueyonder.co.uk
Qualifications and experience:
Diploma in Book and Periodical
Publishing (1984). 20 years'
experience in the promotion, publicity
and sales departments of publishing
houses in Scotland and London;
lecturing experience at Napier
University, Edinburgh (Book
Marketing). 12 years' freelance.
Equipment: Apple Macintosh
desktop publishing system, printing
(colour and b/w) and scanning
facilities. Extensive UK media
database.
Services offered: Promotional
campaigns (media interviews, press
coverage, author tours, direct mail
and advertising) tailored to an
individual author or a publisher's list.
Publicity mailings and preparation of
review lists. Event planning and
sponsorship investigation.
Catalogues, advance information
sheets and press releases written and
designed.

Recent projects include: Publicist
for Alexander McCall Smith; events
diary for Michael Morpurgo; publicity
and promotion for Polygon, Birlinn,
Saltire Society; project management
for Scottish Book Trust including
words@work; event and project
management and publicity for
Scottish Arts Council Book of the Year
Awards; publicity for Saltire Scottish
Literary Awards.

Services

Photo libraries

SUE ANDERSON ABIPP ARPS
Island Focus
12 Pony Park, Benderloch
Oban, Argyll PA37 1SA
Scotland
Tel/Fax: 01631 720078
Mobile: 07799 693619 or 07836
751802
E-mail: info@islandfocus.co.uk
Web site: www.islandfocus.co.uk
Qualifications and Experience:
Professional photographers (freelance
& qualified as above) specialising in
landscape, illustrative, multi media
and PR. Co-author and illustrator of
various publications over last 20
years.
Founder member: www.aim-hi.org
Services offered: Comprehensive
Scottish stock photo library –
panoramic 6x17cm to 35mm format –
digitised and on line in 2006. CD and
originals available. Commissions
welcome. Location scout and
management and stills photography
for film, video and TV. Distance no
object.

GLASGOW MUSEUMS PHOTO LIBRARY
The Burrell Collection
Pollok Country Park
2060 Pollokshaws Road
Glasgow G43 1AT
Tel: 0141 287 2595
Fax: 0141 287 2585
E-mail:
photolibrary@cls.glasgow.gov.uk
Web site:
www.glasgowmuseums.com
Qualifications and experience:
Knowledgeable staff and competitive
rates
Equipment and Services offered:
Large format colour transparencies,
black and white photographic prints,
digital images of over 15,000 images
of works held in Glasgow City
Council's 13 museums.

NATIONAL GALLERIES
OF SCOTLAND

NGS Picture Library
The Dean Gallery
73 Belford Road
Edinburgh EH4 3DS
Contact: Shona Corner
Tel: 0131 624 6260
Fax: 0131 623 7135
E-mail:
picture.library@nationalgalleries.org
Web site: www.nationalgalleries.org
The National Galleries of Scotland
(NGS) Picture Library can supply
colour transparencies and black and
white photographs of over 30,000
works from the National collection. A
selection of works from the collection
are also available as digital images.

Fine art images from the
Renaissance to the present day are
available and covering a wide range of
subjects including landscape, still life,
animals, genre, costume and
portraits. We have the world's finest
collection of Scottish art, a large
collection of Surrealist works, and
extensive holdings of early
photography and old master
paintings.

The NGS collections are now
available to search online via our web
site www.nationalgalleries.org

We supply a vast array of images
to a wide range of clients throughout
the world and are happy to deal with
any enquiries – however vague.

Services

Print and production

BERCKER UK LTD
88 Kingsway, Holborn,
London, WC2B 6AA
Tel: +44 (0) 207 726 7200
Fax: +44 (0) 207 841 1001
E-mail: charlie.tait@bercker.co.uk
Web site: www.bercker.co.uk
Contact: Charlie Tait
Services offered: Bercker is a privately owned book printer based in Kevelaer, Germany.

We print high quality text and illustrated books on papers ranging from 28gsm bible stock to 130gsm coated cartridge.

Your books can be sewn or unsewn as a cased, paperback, pvc or a flexi-bound product. Additional finishing processes include covers with flaps, multiple ribbon markers, head and tail bands, foil blocking, embossing, die-cutting, stickering in-line, thumb indexing, drilling and colour edging plus 'binding-in' CD's and postcards.

Quality is the guiding principle of Bercker's philosophy, and we put that commitment to quality into every stage of the book production process.

CROMWELL PRESS LTD, THE

Aintree Avenue,
White Horse Business Park,
Trowbridge, Wiltshire BA14 0XB
Tel: 01225 711 400
Fax: 01225 711 429
E-mail: sales@cromwellpress.co.uk
Web site: www.cromwellpress.co.uk
Mobile: 07967591771
Contact: John Turner
Services offered: Cromwell Press
specialise in the manufacture of
books, journals, loose-leaf, cased &
limp mono and two colour printing
and cover jacket production.
See display advertisement p.152

DIGISOURCE GB LTD

12 Dunlop Square,
South West Deans Industrial,
Livingston, West Lothian, EH54 8SB
Tel: +44 (0) 1056 463046
Fax: +44 (0)1056 463146
E-mail:
yvonne.cochrane@digisource.co.uk
Web site: www.digisource.co.uk
Contact: Yvonne Cochrane
Digisource has been trading since
1997. We are one of Great Britain's
leading providers of digital
print-on-demand to the computer,
telecommunications, financial,
medical, education, local government
and publishing market sectors. Our
flexibility, speed and quality allow us
to develop unique Just-In-Time
printing solutions which are
economical to our customers'
requirements. Our print model fits well
with markets where lengthy print runs
are not required and our pricing
structure is very competitive with
short to medium print runs. We also
print marketing literature and offer
various types of in-house finishing
such lamination, perforation, perfect
binding, saddle stitching and wire-o
binding.

SCOTPRINT

Gateside Commerce Park,
Haddington,
East Lothian EH41 3ST
Tel: 01620 828800
Fax: 01620 828801
E-mail: ngray@scotprint.co.uk
Web site: www.scotprint.co.uk
Mobile: 07966 531105
Contact: Norrie Gray
Services offered: Single, two- and
four- colour books produced
computer to plate on large format
presses. In-House Binding including,
Wire Stitch, Sewn and Slotted.

Services

Sales

BOOKSPEED
16 Salamander Yards,
Edinburgh EH6 7DD
Tel: 0131 467 8100
Fax: 0131 467 8008
E-mail: sales@bookspeed.com
Web site: www.bookspeed.com
Company established: 1986
Contacts: Kingsley Dawson (Sales
Director) Shona Rowan (Marketing
and Bibliographic Manager)
Services offered: Suppliers of
books to retailers of all sizes including
gift shops, museums, galleries and
visitor attractions. Individual stock
selection for customers from a
database of 500,000 titles, on all
subjects, at all prices for adults and
children alike.

SEOL LTD
West Newington House,
10 Newington Road,
Edinburgh EH9 1QS
Tel: 0131 668 1456
Fax: 0131 668 4466
E-mail: info@seol.ltd.uk
Contact: Hugh Andrew
Company comprises: Hugh
Andrew, Carol Crawford, Harry Ward,
Len Weir, Carole Hamilton and Helen
Young (Sales Administrator)
Services offered: Representation to
the trade in Scotland. The only sales
force to cover Scotland from Shetland
to Stranraer, with five of the most
experienced reps in the Scottish
trade. Seol has the most extensive
customer base of any sales force
outside wholesale.

Services

Distribution

BOOKSOURCE
50 Cambuslang Road
Cambuslang
Glasgow G32 8NB

Customer Services/Orders:
Tel: 0845 370 0067
(International: +44 845 370 0067)
Fax: 0845 370 0068
(International: +44 845 370 0068)

Finance & Administration:
Tel: 0845 370 0063
(International: +44 845 370 0063)
Fax: 0845 370 0064
(International: +44 845 370 0064)

E-mail: info@booksource.net
Web site: www.booksource.net
Established: 1995
Contacts: Davinder Bedi (Managing Director), Lavinia Drew (Credit Controller), Louise Wilson (Client Services Manager), David Warnock (Operations Manager), Derek Withers (Customer Services Manager).
Description of services:
Established in 1995, BookSource offers warehousing and worldwide distribution services to book trade publishers, charities and funded institutions and other commercial enterprises. BookSource is committed to providing quality of delivery and service, giving our client the competitive edge.

The unique set up of BookSource, with the SPA as majority shareholder, also allows for a greater amount of investment in our resources. We offer all the client services you would expect from a top-class distributor and we pride ourselves on our flexible and responsive approach.

Our commitment to quality of service is apparent in customer and client care. Many of our key personnel have been with BookSource since we started, demonstrating our commitment to our staff and their continuing enthusiasm for what we do.

Writing

Top inside tips from Scottish publishers that could help get you published

For the last three years the Scottish Publishers Association has run events on getting published at the Edinburgh International Book Festival. Leading publishers, with literary agent Jenny Brown, revealed their answers to frequently asked questions from writers – both published and those seeking discovery. We reproduce here, by kind permission of the EIBF, succinct points made by Jamie Byng, Publisher, Canongate Books, Booker prize winner of 2002 with *Life of Pi* ; Christian Maclean, Manager, Floris Books (Mind, Body and Spirit; Children's); Bill Campbell, Mainstream Publishing (General non-fiction, Sport), Lesley Taylor, Publisher, NMS Enterprises Ltd – Publishing (scholarly and non-fiction); Ali Bowden, Edinburgh University Press, and Sarah Mitchell, Leckie and Leckie (past papers, revision guides and educational).

How do I get an agent, they seem so elusive?

Jenny Brown:

"An agent picks a publisher and negotiates payment, rights, even film and serialisation deals, and takes about 10-15 per cent commission. As many publishers won't look at unsolicited manuscripts, it's wise to get an agent. Try the *Directory of Publishing* in Scotland (Scottish Publishers Association £9.99); *The Writers' and Artists' Yearbook* (A&C Black, £13.99); the Scottish Publishers Association web site

(www.scottishbooks.org) and check the book you are reading! Writers usually thank their agent at the start, so the book in your hand is a good guide to who handles whom. At present 70% of the manuscripts sent to me is fiction, and there aren't many fiction publishers in Scotland. To be successful, try to think about what's selling now – history with parallels to today, for example. However, recently a London publishing fiction commissioning agent said to me that 'glamour is back' and I wondered how that info gets to writers, so it's also a question of staying in touch, and luck. Bear in mind, the average novelist earns under £7,000 a year, and recent figures showed that 85% of writers earn under £20,000 a year."

What is selling in bookshops at the moment?

Jenny Brown:

"Non-fiction dominates the book market in the UK; two out of three books sold in this country are non-fiction. There is a growing appetite for non-fiction, but room in the market for originality. One of the recent trends in non-fiction recently has been narrative non-fiction. This is an increasingly popular form, but there are opportunities for development in this sector. As an agent I advise authors on their work, and try to place the texts with suitable publishing houses. I receive many fiction works but am hungry to see works of non-fiction."

What do you look for in a manuscript that makes you publish it?

Jamie Byng:

"Passion. Canongate's list is primarily fiction, and there's a different decision process to publishing non-fiction. You are not trying to fill gaps with fiction publishing, and it does not have a defined audience as, say, history does. Canongate buy a lot of books in translation, so this makes a different process for decision making. The majority of work sent in to Canongate is mostly clichéd. A manuscript needs to be more than that to be worth the energy that gets put in to make a book a success. Canongate gets 30 – 40 manuscripts a week and will only publish 30 originals and 30 more vertical books (which means previously published in hardback) a year. So as a publisher we need to use our instinct, and if nothing stands out as original thought, or original expression in a manuscript, we pass on it. We pass on most things. It's different with non-fiction – eg a new work on Robert Louis Stevenson, as there might be something new on his life and work and there will be a defined market for it. 20 per cent of the Canongate list is non-fiction, and a good percentage of that is music. The market is defined, but with fiction, as shown with *Life of Pi*, (the Booker Prize winner), it's boundless. We are about to sell a million copies, which shows novels can go beyond any defined market.

For a manuscript that is 'worth publishing', we are guided by the instinctive sense that it's worth reading and we need to feel it has something unique. We need to take it to head offices in Waterstone's and Smiths, and to publishing offices abroad to sell it. There is intense competition for a new work of fiction. So the work has to be an intense piece of work to get a buzz going. Every book chain buys centrally now, so if the writer isn't passionate about it, and if we, the publishers, can't convey that passion to a major chain, or foreign publisher, or convince a literary editor to devote 1000 words in a column to it – no one else can."

What tips would you give to a non-fiction writer?

Jenny Brown:

"Research is essential: what new information or perspective can you add to the canon of a particular subject? It is important to be alive to trends and key events, such as centenaries of subjects, etc. When presenting or sending a manuscript, include a succinct synopsis. Be realistic about your target audience. If your book is on a local subject matter, and would appeal mainly to a local audience, your manuscript is more unlikely to be un-agented."

Sarah Mitchell:

"Focus on a relevant publisher. Research the publisher using the *Directory of Publishing in Scotland*, web sites and the *Writers' and Artists' Yearbook*.

Focus your proposal. Explain the market to the publisher. What is the rationale behind your publication? What level of reader is it aimed at? What ability of audience is it for? Which curriculum does it follow?

Send a summary, contents page and sample material.

Be prepared to listen to your publisher and to adapt your work.

I estimate that for every book Leckie and Leckie publish, a salary is spent, so we must be making a sound investment."

Bill Campbell:
"Presentation is really important. Only about 25% of the books that we publish are agented, so we expect authors to sell themselves. If a writer is expecting a publisher to sell their work, they must be expected to 'sell' themselves. Your publisher becomes your partner – authors must make it easy for publishers. Essentially, as an author, you must put effort into your proposal. You need to be original. Also, do not e-mail manuscripts to publishing companies, or cold-call editors, as their time is precious. Do not submit the same manuscript to a publisher twice – even if the manuscript has been altered."

Lesley Taylor:
"Do your homework, which means do your research. NMS have a core list, but we also do external publishing. So if you are writing about a piece – binoculars or vases – go to the Museum of Scotland and research it. Research an institution's web site before approaching it. Note that some museums only display some of their collection at a time but they still want to give information on a topic, so find out who the curator is and contact them. Tailor your ideas to fit an institution. There is massive scope at the NMS – costume, war, flight. And find out about the corporate strategy. Also, be kind to the institution. If you have an idea, find out who the publisher is, and submit your synopsis, as it may be that something is planned for later, eg an exhibition in three years' time and they do not have an author. It's better to do this, and save everyone's time, rather than to send in a manuscript that the institution can do nothing with."

Any other general advice on writing, please?
Ali Bowden:
"Writing can be a lonely occupation, and it is important for writers to tap into the valuable network of resources that are available – especially those things found in the *Writers' and Artists' Yearbook*. In Scotland, the Scottish Book Trust is a useful centre for information, as is the Society of Authors.

Amazon is a brilliant research tool for writers and publishers. It is crucial to do research before you approach a publishing house, as publishers are incredibly busy.

Build a portfolio. If you are writing

non-fiction, try to get articles published in relevant journals or magazines. This shows the publisher that you have the ability to convey your points concisely.

Try to include a competition analysis with any proposal that you send. This is an excellent tool, and shows the publisher that you have thoroughly researched your market.

Include your CV with your proposal, if it is relevant to the topic and manuscript. If you include it, do keep your covering letter simple."

Are children's publishers all looking for the next J K Rowling?

Christian Maclean:
"Children's publishing at present is overshadowed by J K Rowling. It's true that the Harry Potter books inspired children to read, but the downside is many people now think they must write a children's book and become rich. Last time this kind of phenomenon happened was with Dickens, so bear in mind that average children's novel, if published in hardback might only have sales of 1000 copies (because libraries buy so little) – and in paperback, the sales might only be 2-3,000. So try to bear in mind how the costs stack up when thinking about an advance, or royalty.

Floris have an active children's publishing list called Kelpies. This is aimed at the 8 – 12 age group and we look for a content that is predomi-nantly Scottish, with situations and characters to which modern children can relate. We are not looking for historical fiction, and anti-English sentiment needs to be put into context or avoided. We aim at a wide audience so the content needs to travel. We also avoid Scottish clichés and if Scots is to be used, please note that many children struggle with books written in Scots English. Although Floris publish illustrated children's books, we take these from publishers abroad mostly, so do not accept children's picture book submissions. Send in to us a brief synopsis and the first three chapters of the work with an SAE for the Kelpies list."

And finally …

When submitting a manuscript, remember:
- use A4 paper
- double space
- leave wide margins
- number pages
- start each chapter on a new page
- clearly mark your name and address on the manuscript
- keep illustrations and diagrams separate
- keep a copy of the typescript

You should also include:
- a letter, detailing the outline of the book, the readership you expect it to have, what is special about your work, your qualifications and experience
- a sample chapter
- a full outline of the contents
- an SAE

Getting published

A writer's view *Frederick Lindsay*

There is no mystery about what writers need from publishers. They ask only that the publisher accepts a book, sells a great many copies of it and divides the proceeds fairly and promptly. Unfortunately, as many writers experience the process, it tends to seize up at one stage or another – for the unluckiest at the first.

Relations with an author may begin by the publisher identifying and approaching a writer to whom he/she will offer a commission. More typically, the process will be initiated by the submission of a typescript. The writer will form a poor opinion of a publisher who takes an inordinate time before offering a response. Whatever the difficulties, the limit case in testing a publisher's efficiency and courtesy must surely involve the unsolicited manuscript, of which a dispropor-tionate number containing the widest variation in quality will be from writers of fiction.

It was Bernard Shaw who, in the course of reviewing a publisher's autobiography, claimed that 'a publisher is an infatuated book fancier who cannot write, and an author is an infatuated book fancier who can'. In a period when we are given to understand the balance of power in large publishers has shifted heavily from the editor to the accountant and the sales manager, it would be a welcome leavening if new publishers were to be motivated by a love of books.

As for being able to write, the desktop publisher may well now be a writer who begins with his own work before moving on to publish that of others. The range of those possible others is wide: the literary novelist, the compiler of guide-books, the maker of textbooks. Certainly, not all of them will be 'infatuated book fanciers'. To a surprising extent, however, the same factors will determine whether or not they think well of their publisher.

Not all of these factors will be contractual, but the basis for a harmonious relationship between writer and publisher will be a contract which unambiguously defines the rights and responsibilities on either side. The overwhelming desire of new writers to see their work in print can make them poor judges of their own long-term interests. The new publisher whose aim is a mature business will, on balance, probably be better served in most cases by limiting the advantage taken of this.

In the same way that the publisher starting out will be advised to make use of a professional association, so no difficulty should be felt about dealing with a writer who has the good sense to do the same from the outset. Both parties could do worse than take a look at the Minimum Terms Agreement drawn up by the Society of Authors and accepted by a growing list of publishers as a model of fair dealing.

The single most important item in a contract is the treatment of

Frederick Lindsay is a full-time novelist and writer of scripts for radio, television and film. He was formerly Chairman of the Society of Authors.

copyright. Unless there is good reason otherwise, which should be explained and justified, the author should be expected to license – not sell – his/her copyright in the work. The term of the license and the conditions under which it may be modified and terminated by either party should be dealt with explicitly.

The amount and nature of the editing a work receives will set the tone of the writer's relationship with the publisher. A publisher just setting out may also have to discharge the editing function. If so, it would be strange if the editing was not governed by positive feeling towards a typescript he/she had chosen. By the same token, when editors are employed it would be natural to assume their best work would be done when they are not out of sympathy with the typescript and are clear about the primacy of respecting the writer's intentions. That might seem axiomatic, but every large-scale survey among writers highlights it as an area of concern. At a more mundane level, the writer should be given the opportunity to respond to copy-editing and to check page proofs for any typesetter's errors.

The design of the jacket has such an influence upon sales that it would seem only courteous to at least give the writer a chance to offer an opinion. The copy for the jacket will in most cases benefit from the writer's input; if in nothing else but to check on its accuracy about facts.

Another frequently recorded complaint is directed at the publicity and promotion which a publisher provides to launch a book. There may well be understandable reasons why both have to be limited. It would seem good policy to explain at an early stage what the constraints will be. If then what is promised is done, the writer may still wish it could be more but is likely to give what credit may be due.

Independent auditing of large and small publishers throws up examples of writers not being paid money to which they were entitled. It is more than seventy years since the novelist W B Maxwell lamented 'the publisher's besetting sin of silence'. As with any other business transaction, transparency is the best protection against worries about incompetence or sharp practice. It is in the publisher's interest to provide the writer with proper accounting of print runs, sales and sub-licensing agreements.

In the honeymoon period, the publisher should ply the author with free copies, as many as the contract stipulates. If the bloom fades, he should remember that books should not be remaindered without first offering them to the author at remaindered prices. As for divorce, the best way of avoiding that is to sell the maximum possible number of books – which is supposed, after all, to be the point of the exercise.

Prizes and awards

ANGUS BOOK AWARD

Moyra Hood,
Educational Resources Service
Librarian, Bruce House,
Wellgate, Arbroath DD11 3TL
Tel: 01241 435 045
Fax: 01241 435 034
E-mail: cularbers@angus.gov.uk
Qualifying period: July–June of previous year
Presentation date: May
Value: Winner receives £500 and the Award trophy, which takes the form of a replica of the Pictish Aberlemno Serpent stone.
Frequency: Annual by nomination from Angus teachers and librarians
Description: Sponsored by Angus Council, the award is open to authors resident in the UK, for the best paperback novel for teenagers, published in the qualifying period. The shortlist of five is chosen by a group of teachers and librarians with input from pupils, but the final decision is made by some 400 pupils from selected third-year classes in all eight Angus Secondary Schools. An important aspect of the award is the participation of the pupils in an evening ceremony attended by the short-listed authors, at which the winner is announced.

C B OLDMAN PRIZE

Mr R Turbet,
Special Libraries & Archives,
University of Aberdeen,
King's College,
Aberdeen AB24 3SW
Tel: 01224 274 266
Fax: 01224 273 891
E-mail: r.turbet@abdn.ac.uk
Presentation date: Easter
Value: £200
Frequency: Annual competition
Description: Awarded by UK branch of the International Association of Music Libraries for the year's best book of music bibliography, librarianship or reference by an author domiciled in UK.

JAMES TAIT BLACK MEMORIAL PRIZES

University of Edinburgh,
Department of English Literature,
David Hume Tower,
George Square,
Edinburgh EH8 9JX
Tel: 0131 650 3619
Fax: 0131 650 6898
E-mail: S.Strathdee@ed.ac.uk
Web site:
www.englit.ed.ac.uk/jtbinf.htm
Final entry date: 31 January
Presentation date: June
Value: Two prizes of £10,000 each
Frequency: Annual competition
Description: One prize for fiction and one for biography, or work of that nature, first published in Britain in the previous calendar year from the 1st of January to the 31st of December.

ROBERT LOUIS STEVENSON FELLOWSHIP

The Administrator,
RLS Memorial Award,
National Library of Scotland,
George IV Bridge,
Edinburgh EH1 1EW
Tel: 0131 623 3762
Fax: 0131 623 3702
E-mail: b.blacklaw@nls.uk
Web site: www.nls.uk
Final entry date: see web site for details
Qualifying period: N/A
Contact: Marketing Services
Presentation date: January
Value: Travel, living expenses & accommodation
Frequency: Annual competition
Description: The RLS Memorial Award provides the winners with a two-month residency at the Hotel Chevillon International Arts Centre in Grez-sur-Loing, near Fontainbleau in France, during March/April and November/December. It is supported by the Scottish Arts Council and the National Library of Scotland. Applications are invited from writers born or resident in Scotland, who have completed their full-time education. Writers in all fields may apply but preference may be given to those specialising in fiction, poetry and travel writing – including writing for children.

ROYAL MAIL AWARDS FOR SCOTTISH CHILDREN'S BOOKS, ADMINISTRATED BY BRAW IN PARTNERSHIP WITH THE SCOTTISH ARTS COUNCIL

Anna Gibbons, Manager, BRAW Scottish Book Trust, Sandeman House, Trunk's Close, 55 High Street, Edinburgh, EH1 1SR

Tel: 0131 524 0160
Fax: 0131 524 0161
E-mail: anna.gibbons@scottishbooktrust.com
Web site: www.braw.org.uk
Final entry date: 31 January
Qualifying period: January–December
Presentation date: December
Value: £4,200 in total; £1,000 for the winner in each category and £200 each for runners up

Description: Awards are given to new and established authors of published books in recognition of high standards of writing for children in three age group categories: younger children (0-7 yrs), younger readers (8-12 yrs), older readers (13-16 yrs). Shortlist drawn up by panel of children's book experts and then winner in each category decided by children and young people voting for their favourites in book groups in schools and libraries across Scotland. Authors should be Scottish or resident in Scotland, but books of particular Scottish interest by other authors are eligible for consideration. Posthumous awards cannot be made. Guidelines available on request.

SALTIRE SOCIETY SCOTTISH LITERARY AWARDS

The Saltire Society,
9 Fountain Close,
22 High Street,
Edinburgh EH1 1TF

Tel: 0131 556 1836
Fax: 0131 557 1675
E-mail: kathleen@saltiresociety.org.uk
Web site: www.saltiresociety.org.uk
Final entry date: End of August
Presentation date: 30 November
Scottish Book of the Year: Value £5,000, sponsored by The Faculty of Advocates.
Scottish First Book of the Year by a New Author: Value £1,500, sponsored by Royal Mail.
Frequency: Annually through Saltire Award Panels

Description: Book of the Year: for a book on or about Scotland, or for a book with Scottish connections, not necessarily written by a Scot.
First book of the Year: as above.

SCOTTISH ARTS COUNCIL BOOK AWARDS

Gavin Wallace, Head of Literature
Scottish Arts Council,
12 Manor Place, Edinburgh EH3 7DD
Tel: 0131 226 6051
Fax: 0131 225 9833
E-mail:
gavin.wallace@scottisharts.org.uk
Web site: www.scottisharts.org.uk
The Scottish Arts Council Book
Awards are currently undergoing
reconfiguration, and will be re-
launched in 2007. Please contact the
Literature Department should further
information be required.

SCOTTISH HISTORY BOOK OF THE YEAR

The Saltire Society, 9 Fountain Close,
22 High Street, Edinburgh EH1 1TF
Tel: 0131 556 1836
Fax: 0131 557 1675
E-mail: kathleen@saltiresociety.org.uk
Web site: www.saltiresociety.org.uk
Final entry date: End of June
Presentation date: 30 November
Value: £1,500
Frequency: Annually, by nomination
from professors of Scottish history
and editors of historical journals.
Description: For a published work of
Scottish historical research (including
intellectual history and the history of
science). Editors of texts are not
eligible.

*Sponsored by
Gillespie Macandrew WS*

SALTIRE SOCIETY, SCOTTISH RESEARCH BOOK OF THE YEAR

The Saltire Society,
9 Fountain Close,
22 High Street,
Edinburgh EH1 1TF
Tel: 0131 556 1836
Fax: 0131 557 1675
E-mail: kathleen@saltiresociety.org.uk
Web site: www.saltiresociety.org.uk
Final entry date: End of August
Presentation date: 30 November
Value £1,500
Frequency: Annually through Saltire Award Panels
Description: For a work, which adds to our knowledge and understanding of Scotland and the Scots. Books should offer new insight or add a new dimension to the subject.

Sponsored by
The National Library of Scotland

TESS/SALTIRE SOCIETY PRIZE FOR EDUCATIONAL PUBLICATION

The Saltire Society,
9 Fountain Close,
22 High Street,
Edinburgh EH1 1TF
Tel: 0131 556 1836
Fax: 0131 557 1675
E-mail: kathleen@saltiresociety.org.uk
Web site: www.saltiresociety.org.uk
Final entry date: end of January
Presentation date: end of April
Value: certificates only
Frequency: Annually by nomination through publishers.
Description: For an example of a published non-fiction work which enhances the teaching and learning of an aspect of the curriculum in Scottish schools.

Sponsored by The Times Educational Supplement in Scotland.

Poetry

Getting your poetry published *Robyn Marsack*

We should warn you at the outset that this is a difficult business!

It may be that the main audience for your poems is essentially your family and friends, or a wider circle in the local community. If this is the case, and you are willing to publish a booklet or pamphlet yourself, look at a few poetry books first, and see how they are set out; type up the text on a word-processor, and get costs for duplicating, folding and stapling from a reputable local reprographic firm. Sensible advice on doing this is available in the *Writers' & Artists' Yearbook*, which you can consult in most public libraries. Its sections on poetry and on self-publishing are strongly recommended reading. You could also check out the pamphlet web site at: http://scottish-pamphlet-poetry.com.

If you are serious about a general audience for your work, then initially the best route to publication is through the small literary magazines, of which the Scottish Poetry Library has a good selection in its journals section on the mezzanine floor. You can consult the SPL webpages for a list of the magazines we subscribe to at: www.spl.org.uk/browse_periodicals.html. The Library also has a small selection of Scottish magazines for sale.

If you live outside the Edinburgh area, you may find some of these magazines for sale in specialist bookshops. The SPL can provide you with a list of magazines that accept poetry (send an A4/A5 SAE).

In order to match what you write to a suitable magazine publisher, it is essential to read a variety of journals to form an idea of the kind of work they will accept. Send no more than 4-6 poems, with an SAE, and expect to wait about a month for a reply.

Again, if you are approaching a publisher, it is essential to know what kind of books they publish to be sure that your kind of poetry is their kind of poetry. The SPL is an obvious resource, and we do send books out on postal loan (our catalogue is available online at: www.spl.org.uk/browse_catalogue.html). If you are looking to publish a collection of poems, especially in Scotland, we recommend that you consult the following books (as well as *The Writers' & Artists' Yearbook*, and *The Writers' Handbook*), as each publisher has different requirements:

The Directory of Publishing in Scotland

Scottish Publishers Association
137 Dundee Street
Edinburgh EH11 1BB
Tel: 0131 228 6866
Web site:
www.scottishbooks.org/about/index

The Small Press Guide

Writers' Bookshop
Remus House, Coltsfoot Drive
Woodston, Peterborough PE2 9JX
Tel: 01733 898101
Web site: www.forwardpress.co.uk

Literary journals and publications

ARTWORK

PO Box 3, Ellon,
Aberdeenshire AB41 9EA
Tel: 01651 842429
Fax: 01651 842180
ISDN: 01651 843900
Advertising contact: Sandra Moore
Tel/fax: 01436 673327
E-mail: artwork@famedram.com
Web site: www.artwork.co.uk
Contacts: Bill Williams (Publisher);
Sandra Moore (Advertising); Eleanor
Stewart (Production)
Publication frequency: Bi-monthly
Title established: 1983
Description of contents: The
north's arts newspaper distributed to
arts centres and galleries throughout
Scotland and into the north of
England, with an increasingly active
web site featuring lively desk TV
interviews.

CHAPMAN
(Scotland's Quality
Literary Magazine)

4 Broughton Place,
Edinburgh EH1 3RX
Tel: 0131 557 2207
Fax: 0131 556 9565
E-mail:
chapman-pub@blueyonder.co.uk
Web site: www.chapman-pub.co.uk
Contact: Joy Hendry (editor),
Edmund O' Connor (assistant editor)
Company established: 1970
Titles in print: 60
Publication frequency: Three times
a year
Price: £6.30 (inc p&p);
subscription £20.00 (1 year);
£37.00 (2 years)
Description of contents: A literary
magazine featuring poetry, short
stories, articles, reviews and
commentary on cultural and artistic
affairs. The emphasis is on Scotland
but also international, including
translation. Each issue has a special
featured artist, previous ones being
Jack Vettriano, John Bellany and
Sheila Mullen.
Instructions for contributors:
Submissions welcome (must be
accompanied by a SAE). Write or
e-mail for guidelines.

DARK HORSE, THE

c/o 3-B Blantyre Mill Road,
Bothwell, South Lanarkshire G71 8DD
E-mail: gjctdh@freenetname.co.uk
Web site:
http://www.star.ac.uk/darkhorse.html
Contact: Gerry Cambridge (Editor)
Title established: 1995
Publication frequency: Two
times a year
Price: £3.00. Subscription (three
issues) £11.00. All cheques payable
to 'Dark Horse Writers'
Description of contents: Critical
essays and polemic on contemporary
poetry; interviews; in-depth reviews;
poetry (with an emphasis on work in
metre or rhyme; free verse of quality
also included).
Instructions for contributors:
Essays and reviews usually solicited;
writers interested in supplying such
material please query first. Poems:
four to six poems, with name and
address on each page and a SAE.
Poets should have carefully read the
magazine before submitting.
Payment: contributors' copy.

LALLANS MAGAZINE

Scots Language Society
Blackford Lodge, Blackford
Perthshire PH4 1QP
Tel: 01764 682315
Fax: 0845 428 5086
E-mail: mail@lallans.co.uk
Web site: www.lallans.co.uk
Contacts: John Law (Editor)
Publication frequency: Twice
annually
Price: £6.50 (Annual subscription
£12)
Description of contents: Writings in
Scots on cultural matters; creative
prose and poetry.
Instructions for contributors:
Electronic copy preferred by e-mail
or disk – RTF format if possible.

NEW WRITING SCOTLAND

Dept of Scottish Literature,
7 University Gardens,
University of Glasgow,
Glasgow G12 8QH
Tel: 0141 330 5309
Contact: Duncan Jones
E-mail: office@asls.org.uk
Web site: www.asls.org.uk
Title established: 1983
Publication frequency: Annually
Price: £6.95

Description of contents: Contains poetry, prose, drama excerpts and short stories in Scots, Gaelic, English by new and established writers.

Instructions for contributors: Must be a writer resident in Scotland or Scots by birth or upbringing. The work must be neither previously published nor accepted for publication. Submissions should be typed on one side of the paper only, and should be accompanied by a covering letter giving your name and address. Your name should not appear on the individual works. If you would like to receive an acknowledgement of receipt, please enclose a stamped addressed postcard. If you would like to be informed if your submission is unsuccessful, or if you would like your submissions returned, you should enclose a stamped addressed envelope with sufficient postage. Submissions are accepted between 1 May and 30 September each year. We are sorry but we cannot accept submissions by fax or e-mail.

POETRY SCOTLAND

diehard publishers,
91-93 Main Street,
Callander FK17 8BQ
Web site: www.poetryscotland.co.uk
Contact: Sally Evans (Editor)
Webmaster: Colin Will
Title established: Originally 1951; new series 1997
Publication frequency: Quarterly
Price: £5.00 for five issues

Description of contents: The best new poetry in English, Scots, Gaelic, sometimes French, Welsh etc. Lively and active web site which also has Open Mouse page to which poems may be sent. Web site for new book information, poetry news, etc

Instructions for contributors: Please take a look at our web site, which includes advice to writers.

PRODUCT
Edinburgh:
PO Box 23071, EH3 5WS
Tel: 0131 558 5449
Glagow:
35a Dalhousie Street
Glasgow G3 6PW
Tel: 0141 332 3738
E-mail: contact@product.org.uk
Web site: www.product.org.uk
Contact: Chris Small/Patrick Small
(Editors)
Title established: 1999
Frequency of publication: Three
times a year
Price: £3.50
Description of contents: General
culture magazine covering Scottish
and international literature, film, music,
visual art and politics. Promotes new
fiction, art and poetry.
Instructions for contributors:
Please contact magazine for
submission guidelines.

SCOTTISH STUDIES REVIEW
c/o Association for Scottish Studies
Literary Studies,
Department of Scottish Literature,
7 University Gardens,
University of Glasgow,
Glasgow G12 8QH
Tel/fax: 0141 330 5309
E-mail: office@asls.org.uk
Contacts: Duncan Jones (General
Manager); Dr Margery Palmer
McCulloch and Professor Murray
Pittock (Editors); Dr Valentina Bold
(Reviews Editor)
Title established: 2000. This
magazine is a continuation of Scottish
Literary Journal and Scotlands.
Publication frequency: Twice yearly
Price: £38.00 (ASLS subscription)
Description of contents: Referred
articles on any aspect of Scottish
literature and culture. Normally one
interview with a major Scottish figure
in each number. Reviews and listings
of Scottish books.
Instructions for contributors:
Guidance notes available from
Duncan Jones or from the ASLS web
site (www.asls.org.uk).

TEXTUALITIES AND TEXTUALITIES.NET

Main Point Books
8 Lauriston Street,
Edinburgh EH3 9DJ
Tel/fax: 0131 228 4837
E-mail: the.editor@textualities.net
Web site: www.textualities.net
Contact: Jennie Renton (Editor)
Title established: 1986 (as Scottish Book Collector)
Publication frequency: Annually and also frequently updated online literary magazine
Price: (annual UK subscription: £14.00 individual/£20.00 organisation) Description of contents: Author interviews, collecting features, history of the book, essays on relationship with books, artists' books.
Instructions for contributors:
Please phone editor in first instance.

VARIANT

1/2 189B Maryhill Road,
Glasgow G20 7XJ
Tel/fax: 0141 333 9522
E-mail: variantmag@btinternet.com
Web site: www.variant.org.uk
Contacts: Leigh French
Title established: Re-launched 1996.
Frequency of publication: Three times a year
Price: Free
Description of contents:
Independent arts and culture magazine; a platform for critical debate and the circulation of challenging ideas utilising both a pulp and on-line presence. Variant promotes debate within cultural areas which are otherwise ignored, hidden, suppressed or censored, working for a greater number of voices to be represented.
Instruction for contributors:
Contact editors for writers' guidelines, (also available on the web site).

VENNEL PRESS

Middle House, 33 Cherry Orchard,
Staines, Middlesex TW18 2DE
E-mail: vennel@hotmail.com
Web site: www.indigogroup.co.
uk/llpp/vennel.html
Contact: Leona Carpenter
Title established: 1990
Frequency of publication: Annual
Description of contents: Modern
Scottish poetry.
Instructions for contributors:
Essential to read a volume first before
submitting work.

WRITERS' NEWS/
WRITING MAGAZINE

First Floor, Victoria House,
143-145 The Headrow,
Leeds LS1 5RL
Tel: 0113 200 2929
Fax: 0113 200 2928
E-mail:
janet.davison@writersnews.co.uk
derek.hudson@writersnews.co.uk
Web site: www.writersnews.co.uk
Contacts: Derek Hudson (Publishing
Editor); Janet Davison (Commercial
Publisher)
Frequency of publication: Writers'
News monthly subscription only;
Writing Magazine monthly, also
available on newsstand.
Price: £44.90 joint subscription UK;
Writing Magazine £3.40 (newsstand)
Description of contents: Writers'
News; journal giving market news,
competitions, members' news etc.
Writing Magazine: how-to features
and interviews with top authors.
Instructions for contributors:
Contact our Leeds office by e-mail

ZED 2 0
Akros Publications,
33 Lady Nairn Avenue,
Kirkcaldy, Fife KY1 2AW
Tel: 01592 651 522
Contact: Duncan Glen
Title established: 1991
Frequency of publication: Annually
Price: £3.95
Description of contents: Poetry,
prose and articles on literature and
the arts.

Getting your fiction published

A first-time writer's experience *Linda Cracknell*

I didn't think about publication when I started writing. It seemed like a distraction from the real business of words. But ultimately I wanted an audience – wanted to know if my writing could make others feel or think or react in some way. This led me up a steep learning curve to the publication of a short story collection, *Life Drawing*[1], and a novel underway which I have confidence will get a fair reading by agents and publishers when the time comes. In 2002, I left another career to become a full-time writer and writer-in-residence.

The three most important things that helped to get me started were: feedback; deadlines; and a serious attitude to my work. Feedback helped me develop confidence; deadlines made me organise my time and push stories right through to polished completion; a serious attitude ensured that I was professional – making time (for the publishing processes as well as the writing itself), researching the field, and setting targets.

Confidence is a huge factor in successful writing, and this can be a vicious circle. Where do you get that confidence from? Well, yes, one important source is from being published. According to a survey undertaken by *Mslexia*[2] magazine, this is a particular problem for women, who are 50% less likely to submit their work for publication than men. So how can we develop confidence and overcome our fears of rejection or appearing self important?

My attitude changed dramatically after winning the *Macallan/Scotland on Sunday* competition in 1998 with my first published story. People started to refer to me as a 'writer' so I had to start thinking of myself as one. Once I recovered from the shock, I decided to prepare a collection of short stories. In order to impress a publisher, I knew that I needed not only the manuscript but also a record of previously published stories.

However, I had only one published story and not a clue about how to get started.

Writing groups were a vital way for me of preparing for the world of print. I gained constructive criticism, contact with people who knew more about publishing than I did, camaraderie through highs and lows. At the very least, a writing group was an audience for the piece of work I took along to discuss, and the meeting provided that all important deadline. One group had its own internal competitions, judged by professional writers who gave us written feedback. Some groups published anthologies to sell to friends and relatives. I got the chance to meet visiting writers.

I sought feedback. I was lucky enough to have Liz Lochead as a first tutor on a residential course. Subsequently I signed up with the *Open College of the Arts*[3] which provided deadlines *and* feedback, negotiated with a personal tutor. I took *Arvon Foundation* courses and attended numerous workshops with

[1] *Life Drawing* by Linda Cracknell, 11:9, 2000, ISBN 1-903238-13-7

[2] *Three cures for mslexia*, Debbie Taylor, *Mslexia*, Issue 1, Spring 1999

[3] Open College of the Arts, Tel 0800 731 2116, www.oca-uk.com

writers. My own local writers-in-residence were a great source of encouragement, commenting on work in progress, and even holding writing classes. All of the above helped me build contacts and get feedback. This was especially useful when I was too inexperienced to judge for myself when a story was publishable.

I looked at my time and prioritised it just as I did for my day job. I dropped any attempt at housework, got rid of the TV, made a filing system so I didn't keep losing competition entry forms. I negotiated a reduction of my working week, and later applied for a few months unpaid leave to start my novel with the support of a Scottish Arts Council bursary.

I got tooled up with books and magazines. *Mslexia* still does it for me – offering practical advice, skills development, and an ear to the ground on publishing opportunities and competitions. I bought the *Writers' and Artists' Yearbook,* and learnt how to submit work formatted properly (even down to what sort of envelope to send for the rejections and returns!). I researched editors' names, noticed who published the kind of work I aspired to, and I drew up a list of targets in terms of competitions (with deadlines) and magazines.

I kept a chart with a running list of all my finished stories. I got into a cycle of completion, submission, and feedback. Every finished story went out again as soon as it bounced back. I learnt to think of rejections as unlucky rather than a signal that I couldn't write – the kinder ones came with suggestions and advice. Occasionally stories were accepted and I even earnt a few pounds.

By the time I was dealing with the sale of a full-length manuscript, I'd had six of the eighteen stories published or broadcast. I felt more like a small business than a writer. As I had no agent, I submitted the manuscript myself, and ended up in negotiation on an offer. I joined the *Society of Authors* and they provided a contract vetting service which helped me through the small print. Then the publishing and marketing machinery started whirring, and, some months later, there was my book.

I had a lucky break by winning a competition so early in my writing career. This won't happen to most writers. But there are other ways of developing contacts and getting to know the world you're trying to penetrate. It's no doubt that taking publishing seriously requires hard work and some business as well as writing skills.

Sometimes the battle to get into print can seem to divide publishers and writers, 'them and us'. When I picked my first precious book up in a shop, knowing that the publisher was determined to get it under the hungry eyes of readers, all the hard work seemed worth it. And it was good to realise that they were on my side. After all, where would publishers be without writers?

Writers' groups

ANGUS WRITERS' CIRCLE

Contact: Mrs Margaret Warren
(Secretary), 9 Craig Terrace,
Ferryden, Montrose DD10 9RE
Tel: 01674 671 238

BERWICK WRITERS' WORKSHOP

Contact: Mary Rawnsley,
c/o The Maltings Arts Centre,
Eastern Lane,
Berwick-upon-Tweed, TD15 1AJ
Tel: 018907 71726 (home number)
E-mail: berwick_writers_workshop@
yahoo.co.uk
We always welcome new members
(novice or experienced); meeting held
fortnightly on alternate Wednesday
evenings or call Mary Rawnsley in first
instance.

BUTE WRITERS' GROUP

Contact: Steve Howrie (Secretary),
Orissor House, Craigmore Road,
Rothesay, Isle of Bute PA20 9LB
Tel: 01700 505 357
Fax: 01700 505 394
E-mail: secy@butewriters.org
Web site: www.butewriters.org

EDINBURGH WRITERS' CLUB

Contact: Ms Margaret McNeill,
Membership Secretary
Tel: 0131 228 3651
Meetings held fortnightly at the
Osbourne Hotel, 53-59 York Place,
Edinburgh. Calls first to the
membership secretary are welcome
and an info pack will be sent out.
Currently recruiting new members.

ERSKINE WRITERS

Contact: Helen Baxter
15 Glen Road, Bishopton PA7 5EJ
Tel: 01505 340 826
E-mail: helen@helenbaxter.ndo.co.uk

FALKIRK WRITERS' CIRCLE

Contact: Ms Isobel Quinn,
73 Alma Street, Falkirk FK2 7QA
Tel: 01324 620 048
E-mail: cdsm520@yahoo.co.uk
Aims and Objectives: Falkirk
Writers' Circle is an independent, self-financing group. It is non-party and non-sectarian. Its objectives are the promotion of a mutual association of writers for the common benefit of all and the encouragement of writing in all its branches. The Club aims to celebrate the best of modern writing. It encourages the highest possible standards of excellence in presentation, use of language and breadth of ideas. The Club also encourages the best of its amateur writers to submit for publication.

Services Provided: The Club employs a professional tutor who gives lectures, advice and sets assignments on up to six evenings in the year; organises challenges and competitions with other writing clubs and circulates information on national writing competitions; distributes information of use to writers such as web addresses, publishers and 'how to' notes on writing techniques. The Club organises occasional speakers and workshops on the art of writing, holds regular social functions with a literature/writing theme and provides mutually supportive positive help on members' current writing.

All writers both new and experienced are welcome.

PERTHSHIRE WRITERS' GROUP

Contact: Alice Walsh (Secretary),
34 Glenfarg Terrace, Perth, PH2 0AP
Tel: 01738 637 931
E-mail:
alice.walsh1@blueyonder.co.uk
Objectives: We use tutors from all disciplines to encourage and enhance all disciplines of writing and we meet to discuss work by members, and to encourage new members in their writing.

THE SCOTTISH ASSOCIATION OF WRITERS

33 Murdiestone Street,
Greenock PA15 4DS
Tel: 01360 770 073
Contacts: Joyce Ward (President);
Joan Fleming (Secretary),
60 Russell Drive, Bearsden,
Glasgow, G61 3BB.
Tel: 0141 9425115
The Association, founded in 1967, promotes and encourages the art and craft of writing in all its forms. Membership is available to groups of writers forming a club or workshop, with the approval of the Association Council and on payment of the annual fee, currently £8.00 per group plus £2.00 per member.

There are currently around 25 member groups, each of which elects a delegate to the Committee of the Association. The main work of the Association is the organisation of an annual Weekend School, usually in March, with a programme of speakers, seminars, competitions and adjudications.

STRATHENDRICK WRITERS' GROUP

Contact: Mrs Deirdre Davidson (Secretary), 1 Burnside, Balfron, Stirlingshire G63 0QQ
Tel: 01360 440 585
E-mail: SDDDatburnside@aol.com
Web site:
www.strathendrickwriters.com
Objectives: We use tutors from all disciplines to encourage and enhance all disciplines of writing and we meet to discuss work by members, and to encourage new members in their writing.

WRITERS' UMBRELLA

14 Ladysgate Court,
Carronshore, Falkirk FK2 8HE
Tel: 01324 570445
E-mail:
barbara@ladysgate.freeserve.co.uk
Contact: Ms B Hammond
The object of the group is to support
writers in their own homes. Members
may be those who write in isolation or
who already belong to a formal group.
The aim of the organisation is to
provide material of interest to writers.
The bi-monthly newsletter includes
news and views, hints and tips and
information on competitions and
opportunities for writers. The Umbrella
has items of interest for poets,
novelists, writers of short-stories and
those who specialise in non-fiction
writing.
Services: Club news, members folio
service, a free entry competition with
cash prize and an annual big money
competition in conjunction with
'Lothian Life' plus occasional
workshops.
Anyone who loves to write is
welcome.

Writers' contacts

**MONIACK MHOR
WRITERS' CENTRE,**
Teavarran, Kiltarlity,
Beauly, Inverness-shire IV4 7HT
Tel: 01463 741 675
E-mail:
m-mhor@arvonfoundation.org
Many disciplines of residential
courses, in association with Arvon in
a beautiful Highland setting.

**PLAYWRIGHTS' STUDIO,
SCOTLAND**
CCA, 350 Sauchiehall Street,
Glasgow, G2 3JD
Tel: 0141 332 4403
Textphone: 0141 332 3208
Fax: 0141 332 6352
Web site:
www.playwrightsstudio.co.uk
Contact: Claire Burkitt (Administrator)
E-mail: info@playwrightsstudio.co.uk
Originally dreamed up by playwright
Tom McGrath, and following extensive
research by Faith Liddell, the Scottish
Arts Council awarded funding to
create the Playwright's Studio,
Scotland in 2004.

Led by Creative director Julie Ellen
and an annually appointed team of
Associate Playwrights, the
Playwrights' Studio is a national arts
organisation designed to celebrate,
promote and develop Scotland's rich
and growing culture for writing and
live performance. It aims to secure a
future for playwrights and their work
by improving and sustaining opportunities and access. Associate
Playwrights for this year are Chris
Hannan, John Clifford and Peter
Arnott. Previous associates are David
Greig, Liz Lockhead and Nicola
McCartney.

Away from the pressure of a
producing theatre, the Playwrights'
Studio, Scotland will place playwrights
at the heart of script development,
tailoring their professional
development to their individual needs.

SCOTTISH SOCIETY OF PLAYWRIGHTS

43 Daisy Street, Flat 2/2,
Glasgow G42 8HG
E-mail: administrator@
scottishsocietyofplaywrights.co.uk
Web site: www.scottishsocietyof
playwrights.co.uk
Chairman: Christopher Deans
SSP is an organisation of professional
playwrights in Scotland. Its purpose is
to negotiate on behalf of, and to
support and promote, the interests of
its members. SSP publishes
*Playwrights Register: A Directory of
Scottish Playwrights* (£4.00 from
SSP at address above).

Writing fellowships

THE SCOTTISH ARTS COUNCIL WRITING FELLOWSHIPS

The Scottish Arts Council funds a series of writing fellowships through-out Scotland in partnership with a wide range of host organisations. The principle behind the fellowships is to invest in writers and writing, and to place literature at the heart of the nation's communities. Fellowships run for a period of one to three years. Fellows devote half of their time to implementing an agreed programme of work in their constituency, and the other half to their own writing. The programme of work usually involves a range of reader / writer development work, developing opportunities for communities to engage with writers, and offering local and national organi-sations the opportunity to promote literature in the community.

Literature Development Officers are funded on the same basis, and undertake important reader and literature development wok in a range of locations around the country. Our aim is to place one Fellow and one Officer in every local authority across Scotland.

Bibliography

Those marked * are available from the SPA's resource library and can be consulted or borrowed by SPA members. The library also stocks magazines and journals such as The Bookseller, Publishing News, Books in Ireland, Chapman, InScotland and Scottish Book Collector.

Book Trade Information

Books and the Consumer: Annual Survey Summary Report (Book Marketing Ltd, London, 2006)

Books as Gifts (Book Marketing Ltd, London. 1991)

The Book Distribution Handbook; Barnard, Michael & Webb, Raymond (Pira International, 1995)*

Book Sales Yearbook 2002, pocket ed. (Whitaker Business Publishing, NP, 2002)*

Books: The International Market 1997 (Euromonitor, London, 1997)

Competition and Choice in the Publishing Industry; Allan, Walter & Curwen, Peter (Institute of Economic Affairs, 1991)*

Household Library Use Survey 1998 (Book Marketing Ltd, London, 1998)

PA Book Trade Yearbook 1990-1999; Fishwick, Francis (Publishers Association, London, available annually)*

UK Book Market 1998-2002 (Market Tracking International Ltd, London, 1998)

UK Printing and Publishing Statistics 1999 (Pira International, Leatherhead, 1999)

UK Publishing (Key Note Publishers, Hampton, 1991)

Verdict on Book Retailers 1998 (Verdict Research Ltd, London, 1998)

World Book Report 1998 (Euromonitor, London, 1998)

World Publishing Monitor (Pira International, 12 issues per annum)

Copyright, Contracts and Rights

Copinger and Skone James on Copyright; Garnett, Rayner James and Davies, 14th ed. (Sweet & Maxwell, London, 1999)

Copyright in a Week; Cornish, Graham (Hodder Arnold, London, 2002)

Copyright, Design and Patents Act 1988 (HMSO, London, 1988)*

Copyright Made Easier; Wall, Raymond A (ASLIB, London, 2000)

Digital Copyright: Protecting Intellectual Property on the Internet; Litman, Jessica (Prometheus, 2006)

Intellectual Property; Bainbridge, David, 5th ed. (Longman, Harlow, 2002)

Publishing Agreements: A Book Of Precedents; Clark, Charles and Owen, Lynette (LexisNexis, London, 2002)

Publishing Law; Jones, Hugh (Routledge, London, March 2002)*

Selling Rights; Owen, Lynette (Routledge, London, 2001)*

Understanding Publishers' Contracts; Legat, Michael (Robert Hale, London, 2002)

A User's Guide to Copyright, 4th ed.; Flint, Michael F (Butterworths, London, 1997)*

Design and Typography

Basic Design and Layout; Swann, Alan (Phaidon, London, 1987)

Creating the Printed Page: A Guide for Authors, Publishers and Designers; Burnett, Robert and Marshall, P. David (British Library Publishing, London, 2003)

Designing Web Usability; Nielson, J (New Riders Publishing, Berkeley, 2000)

The Elements of Typographic Style; Bringhurst, Robert (Hartley & Marks, Vancouver, 1996)

First Steps in Design; Cookman, Brian (Pira International, Leatherhead, 1997)

Making Books – Design in British Publishing Since 1945; Bartram, Alan (The British Library & Oak Knoll Press, London, 1999)*

Methods of Book Design; Williamson, Hugh (Yale University Press, London, 1983)

Print, Editorial, Design & Publishing (Rotovision, NP, 2001)

Printing Type Designs – A New History from Gutenberg to 2000; Glen, Duncan (Akros, Kirkcaldy, 2001)*

The Thames and Hudson Manual of Typography;
Mclean, Ruari (Thames and Hudson, London,
1980)

Directories

Bowker Annual Library and Book Trade Almanac
1999, 4th ed. (Bowker Saur, London, 1999)

Directory of Booksellers Association Members
(The Booksellers Association, London, annual
publication)*

Directory of Members' Services 2006 (Society for
Editors and Proofreaders, London, 2006)*

Directory of Publishing: UK, Commonwealth &
Overseas 2002 (Continuum International
Publishing Group)*

Directory of Publishing Volume 1: United Kingdom
(Cassell/The Publishers Association, London,
annual publication)*

Directory of Scotland's Organisations; Baird, W &
Whittles, K (Whittles Publishing,
Latheronwheel, 1999)*

Freelance Editors and Proofreaders Available
(Society of Freelance Editors and Proofreaders,
London, annual publication)*

Indexers Available (Society of Indexers, London,
annual publication)*

International Book Trade Directory, 3rd ed.
(Bowker Saur, London, 1997)

International Literary Marketplace (PIMS
Directories, NP, 2006)

The Libraries Directory 1996-1998 (James Clarke
and Co., Cambridge, 1998)

Literary Marketplace (PIMS Directories, NP, 2006)*

Picturebook 01: Directory of Children's Illustration
(WaterMark Inc., NP, 2000)

Scottish Library and Information Resources, 12th
ed. (Scottish Library Association, Motherwell,
2000)*

StockIndex 2006 – The Index to specialist stock
libraries (The Publishing Factory Ltd, London,
2006)

Editing and Indexing

Copy-editing – The Cambridge Handbook for
Editors, Authors and Publishers, 3rd ed.;
Butcher, Judith (Cambridge University Press,
Cambridge, 1992)

Developing Editing Skills; Camp, S (McGraw-Hill
Inc., Maidenhead, 2001)

Editing, Design and Book Production; Foster,
Charles (Journeyman, London, 1993)

Editing Fact and Fiction; Sharpe, Leslie and
Gunther, Irene (Cambridge University Press,
Cambridge, 1994)

Editors on Editing – 3rd ed.; Gross, Gerald (Grove
Press, New York, 1993)

The Effective Editor's Handbook; Horn, Barbara
(Pira International, Leatherhead, 1997)

The Fiction Editor: The Novel and the Novelist;
McCormack, Thomas (Sedgewick and
Jackson, 1999)

Indexing, The Art of: A Guide to the Indexing of
Books and Periodicals; Knight, G. Norman
(Allen & Unwin, London, 1979)*

Indexing Books; Mulvany, C. Nancy (University of
Chicago Press, Chicago & London, 2001)

The Oxford Dictionary for Writers and Editors
(Oxford University Press, Oxford, 2000)

The Penguin Writer's Manual; Manser, Martin and
Curtis, Stephen (Penguin, London, 2002)

Proofreading & Editing;Schymkiw, Gunter (Prim-
Ed Publishing, Coventry, 1997)

Electronic Publishing

Books & Publishing on the Internet;
Ferneyhough, Roger (Internet Handbooks,
NP, 2000)

The Electronic Publishing Business and its
Market; Blunden, Brian and Blunden, Margot
(Blueprint, London, 1997)

The Impact of Electronic Publishing – The Future
for Libraries and Publishers; Brown, David J
(Bowker Saur, London, 1999)

The Internet and World Wide Web: The Rough
Guide; Kennedy, Angus J (Penguin, London,
1998)

The Internet: A Writer's Guide (A & C Black,
London, 2000)

An Introduction to Digital Media; Feldman, Tony
(Blueprint/Routledge, London, 1997)

Freelancers

Freelance Copywriting (A & C Black, London,
1999)

Freelance Writing for Newspapers, 2nd ed.; Dick, Jill, (A & C Black, London, 1998)

Indexers Available (Society of Indexers, London, available annually)*

Indexers Available in Scotland (Society of Indexers, Gullane, available annually)

The Society of Freelance Editors and Proofreaders Directory (SFEP, London, available annually)*

Production

The Blueprint Handbook of Print and Production; Barnard, M. et al (Chapman & Hall, 1994)*

Colour Production in a Digital Age; Mortimer, Anthony (Pira International, Leatherhead, 1998)

Colour Proof Correction; Bann, David and Gargan, John (Phaidon, Oxford, 1990)

Colour Reproduction in the Printing Industry; Mortimer, A (PIRA, Leatherhead, 1991)

Dictionary of Printing and Publishing; Collin, P H (Peter Collin Publishing, Teddington, 1997)

Introduction to Pre-Press; Spiers, H (PIRA/NPIF Publishing, 1998)

Introduction to Printing and Finishing: Spiers, H (PIRA/BPIF Publishing, 1998)

Introduction to Printing Technology; Spiers, H (BPIF, 1992)

The Print and Production Manual, 7th ed. (Pira International, Leatherhead, 1998)

The Print Production Handbook; Bann, David (MacDonald Illustrated, London, 1997)*

Publishing Technology Review (Pira International, Leatherhead, 10 issues per annum)

Quality and Productivity in the Graphic Arts; Southworth M & D (Graphic Arts Publishing Co, 1989)

Quality Control for Print Buyers; Green, P (Blueprint, 1992)

Understanding Digital Colour; Green, P (PIRA/BPIF, 2000)

Publicity and Marketing

Are Books Different?; Baverstock, Alison (Kogan Page, London, 1993)*

Author Events – Impact and Effectiveness (Book Marketing Ltd, London)

Benn's Media Directory UK/Europe/World (Benn Business Information, Tonbridge)

Book Promotion, Sales and Distribution: A Management Training Course, (UNESCO, 1991)

The Craft of Copywriting, 2nd ed.; Crompton, Alistair (Century Business, 1995)*

Essentials of Marketing; Blythe, J (Prentice Hall, Harlow, 2005)

How to Market Books, 3rd ed.; Baverstock, Alison (Kogan Page, London, 1999)*

Marketing in Publishing; Forsyth, Patrick (Routledge, Abingdon, 1997)*

Marketing Your Book: An Author's Guide; Baverstock, Alison (A & C Black, London, 2001)

Principles of Direct and Database Marketing; Tapp, Alan (FT Pitman, NP, 1998)*

UK Media Directory (PIMS Directories, 2002)*

Who's Who in the Media 1998 (European Editions plc, 1998)

Willings Press Guide (Reed Information Services, East Grinstead, annual publication)

General Publishing

Book Business; Epstein, Jason (WW Norton and Co., London, 2002)*

Book Facts: An Annual Compendium 1998 (Book Marketing Group, London, 1998)

Bookmaking: A Case Study of Publishing; Dick, Eddie (SFC Media Education)*

Books in the Digital Age; Thompson, John B, (Polity Press, Cambridge, 2006)

The Business of Books; Schiffrin, Andre (Verso Books, New York, 2002)

The Complete Idiot's Guide to Publishing Children's Books; Underdown, Harold (Pearson Professional, Oxford, 2001)

How to Publish your Poetry, 2nd ed. (Allison & Busby, London, 1998)

Imprints in Time: A History of Scottish Publishers Past and Present (Merchiston Publishing, Edinburgh, 1991)*

Inside Book Publishing, 3rd ed.; Clark, Giles (Routledge, Abingdon, 2001)*

Publishing a Book, 3rd ed.; Spicer, Robert (How to Books, 1998)

Publishing in the Information Age; Eisenhart, Douglas, (Praeger, Westport, 1996)*

Publishing for Profit; Woll, Thomas (Kogan Page, London, 2000)

Publishing Now; Owen, Peter (ed), (Peter Owen Publishers, London, 1996)

The Small Press Guide 2002, The Complete Guide to Poetry & Small Press Magazines, 7th ed. (Writers' Bookshop, Peterborough, 2001)*

Writing and Self-Publishing

An Author's Guide to Publishing; Legat, Michael, 3rd ed. (Robert Hale, London, 1998)

The Author's Handbook 1998; Bolt, David (Piatkus Books, London, 1998)

Becoming a Writer; Brande, Dorothea (Jeremy P. Tarcher, Los Angeles, 1981)

Beginner's Guide to Getting Published (Writer's Digest Books, US, 1991)

Bestseller: Secrets of Successful Writing; Brayfield, Celia (Fourth Estate, London, 1997)

Creative Editing: Spot What's Wrong With Your Writing Before an Editor Does; Mackie, Mary (Orion Publishing, London, 1995)

Creative Writing; Doubtfire, Dianne (Hodder Arnold, London, 2003)

501 Writers' Questions Answered; Smith, Nancy (Piatkus Books, London, 1995)

From Pitch to Publication; Blake, Carole (Pan, London, 1999)

Guide to Successful Self-Publishing; Wagner, Steven (Pearson Higher Education, Oxford, 1992)

How to Publish Your Poetry; Finch, Peter (Allison & Busby, Ltd., London 1998)

How to Publish Yourself; Finch, Peter, 2nd ed. (Allison & Busby, Ltd., London, 1997)

How to Write for Publication; McCallum, Chriss, 4th ed. (How To Books, 1997)

How to Write Non-Fiction Books; Wells, Gordon (Writer's Bookshop, 1999)*

If You Want to Write; Ueland, Brenda, 2nd ed. (Graywolf Press, Saint Paul, 1938)

The Oxford Guide to Style (Oxford University Press, 2002)*

The New Oxford Guide to Writing; Kane, Thomas (Oxford University Press, 1994)

Research for Writers, 6th ed.; Hoffman, Ann (A & C Black, London, 2003)

Starting to Write: How to Create Written Work for Publication and Profit; Oliver, Marina, 2nd ed. (Tudor House, NP, 2003)

Teach Yourself Writing Poetry; Sweeney, Matthew & Williams, John (Hodder & Stoughton, London, 1997)

The 38 Most Common Fiction Writing Mistakes: (And How to Avoid Them); Bickham, Jack M. (Writer's Digest Books, NP, 1997)

Understanding Publishers Contracts; Legat, Michael, 2nd ed. (Robert Hale, Ltd., London, 2002)

The Way to Write, 2nd ed.; Fairfax, John & Moat, John (Elm Tree Books, London, 1998)

Word Power: A Guide to Creative Writing; Birkett, Julian, 3rd ed. (A & C Black, London, 1998)

Write and Sell Your Novel; Oliver, Marina, 3rd ed. (How To Books, Oxford, 2003)

The Writers' & Artists' Yearbook (A & C Black, London, annual publication)*

The Writer's Handbook; Turner, Barry (Macmillan/PEN, London, annual publication)

Writer's Handbook; Wells, Gordon, 2nd ed. (Allison & Busby, Ltd., London, 1988)

The Writer's Journey; Vogler, Christopher, 2nd ed. (Pan, London, 1999)

Writers Register 1999 (Scottish Book Trust, Edinburgh, 1999)*

Writing a Play (A & C Black, London, 2001)

Writing Comedy (A & C Black, London 1999)

Writing Down the Bones; Goldberg, Nathalie (Shambhala Publications, Boston, 1988)

Writing for Children, 2nd ed. (A & C Black, London, 1999)

Writing for Television, 3rd ed.; Kelsey, Gerald (A & C Black, London, 1999)

UK Tax Guide for Authors (Ernst & Young, London, published annually)

The Publishing Training Centre at Book House has a mail order service for books on publishing. To obtain the free catalogue, telephone 020 8874 2718 or visit www.train4publishing.co.uk

Index